ABOUT THE AUTHOR

Caroline L. Arnold has been a technology leader
on Wall Street for more than a decade, managing
some of the financial industry's most complex and
visible assignments. She received the Wall Street &
Technology Innovation Award for building the
auction system for the Google IPO, and her name
appears on technology patents and patents pending. Now a managing director at Goldman Sachs
in New York City, Arnold grew up in the San
Francisco Bay Area, received a B.A. in English
literature from the University of California, and
lives in New York City with her husband and
daughter.

SMALL MOVE,

BIG
CHANGE

Using Microresolutions
to Transform
Your Life Permanently

Caroline L. Arnold

PENGUIN LIFE

AN IMPRINT OF

PENGUIN BOOKS

PENGUIN LIFE

UK | USA | Canada | Ireland | Australia
India | New Zealand | South Africa

Penguin Life is part of the Penguin Random House group of companies
whose addresses can be found at global.penguinrandomhouse.com

First published in the United States of America by Viking Penguin,
a member of Penguin Group (USA) LLC, 2014
First published in the United Kingdom by Penguin Life 2016
001

Printed in Great Britain by Clays Ltd, St Ives plc

A CIP catalogue record for this book is available from the British Library

ISBN: 978-0-241-28651-7

www.greenpenguin.co.uk

MIX
Paper from
responsible sources
FSC
www.fsc.org   FSC® C018179

Penguin Random House is committed to a
sustainable future for our business, our readers
and our planet. This book is made from Forest
Stewardship Council® certified paper.

Contents

Contents

Preface

It's late at night as I head up the steep drive to my parents' house, the house I grew up in. I'm just off the plane from New York, and as soon as I cut the engine on my rental car I can hear the crickets chirping in the warm California night. My long day of travel at an end, I let my head fall back against the seat and I listen for a moment. I'm home.

An outside light illuminates the pathway to the front door; inside, the house is dark, my parents asleep. I roll my bag along the pebbled path and slip inside. I'm thirsty, hungry, and tired; my plane was two hours late getting in. But I don't stop for a glass of water or to check what's in the fridge. I go straight to the pantry, open the door, and hang up my car keys on an old brass rack where two other key rings dangle in the dark.

Becoming a licensed driver is a rite of passage in the California suburbs, where you can't really get anywhere without a car. I counted the days to my sixteenth birthday and couldn't wait to get behind the wheel. I learned to hang up the car keys as soon as I came home on the day I passed my driving test—over twenty-five years ago. My new California driver's license meant there would now be three drivers sharing two cars. Keys hidden in purses or pants pockets or tossed onto a bureau meant frustration and lost time. "Hang up the keys!" my parents would shout as soon as I stepped in the door.

But tonight I've arrived in a rental car only I am authorized to drive. My parents each have a car parked in the driveway. We aren't going to share cars, so why hang up the keys? Why bee-line for the hook in the dark?

The answer holds the secret to achieving continuous and sustainable self-improvement. If only I had known the answer all those years ago, every one of my resolutions since would have succeeded.

Introduction: Why Resolutions Fail

I will lose weight.
I will be neat.
I will be on time.
I will get out of debt.
I will be thin by summer.
I will get ahead at work.
I will be more loving.
I will be assertive.
I will get in shape.
I will get organized.
I will quit smoking.
I won't be defensive.
I will be a better person.

Why is it so hard to keep our resolutions? We begin with enthusiasm and determination, yet our will falters and our resolutions fizzle. And every time we break a resolution—a promise we make ourselves to improve our lives—we feel demoralized, powerless to make progress and realize our goals.

Even highly disciplined and successful individuals—*winners*—fail at self-improvement initiatives. We're all losers when it comes to the New Year's resolution, our collective failure rate a spectacular 88 percent. We run in place like hamsters on a wheel, renewing and forsaking the same resolutions in an annual cycle, telling ourselves that if we only had more resolve, more willpower, more *character*, we could force a breakthrough to a better self. We begin each year (or birthday or season or Monday morning) with fresh determination, muster our willpower, tweak our resolutions, and try again. Over time, the pattern of making and breaking resolutions becomes familiar and demoralizing. We go on making resolutions, *but we expect to fail*.

What if instead of failing annually at our New Year's resolutions, we made strategic and targeted resolutions year-round that were guaranteed to succeed and transform us permanently? What if our resolutions brought us immediate rewards, raised our self-awareness, and energized our self-improvement efforts? *What if every time we made a resolution we actually expected to succeed?*

Small Move, Big Change is about making resolutions that succeed every time. By rethinking and refocusing your resolutions, you can master the art of instant and sustainable self-improvement, achieving personal goals that once seemed out of reach. Transparent successes will take the place of mystifying failures, optimism will replace hopelessness, confidence will replace helplessness. You will learn how to succeed instead of fail; indeed, you will learn to *expect* success.

The purpose of this book is to teach you how to translate broad personal goals into *microresolutions* that can be managed, measured, and kept. A microresolution is a compact and powerful commitment designed to nail a precise behavioral target exactly and deliver benefits immediately. Rather than suffering a collapse of willpower after weeks of exhausting effort, you will learn how to overpower your objective through strategic focus and targeted self-control. Your resolutions will pay off the day you start and are sustainable for a lifetime. Microresolutions succeed in every self-improvement category, whether your goal is losing weight, improving a relationship, or saving money.

For most of my life I lived the common experience in resolution making—I failed nearly all the time. These personal failures were a mystery to me, as I was very successful in my career on Wall Street and in nurturing a happy and rewarding family life. I put in long hours running a global department numbering nearly five hundred people, meeting demanding deadlines, and coaching careers; I was devoted to my family, to the needs of my young daughter, husband, and aging parents; I was engaged in charities and active in my community. But despite my capacity to deliver for others and the *take-no-prisoners* attitude I brought to the most challenging career assignments, I struggled to keep the personal commitments I made to myself, from going to the gym regularly to spending more time with my family. With all my energy and determination, I wondered why my resolutions had succeeded only a handful of times.

Finally, after a particularly painful resolution flop, I tried something different. I assigned myself a small but meaningful behavioral change—a *microresolution*—and I succeeded in changing myself immediately and permanently. Yet it was only after succeeding at several more microresolutions modeled on the first that I realized I had stumbled onto a method for making targeted commitments that succeeded virtually every time. I began reaching goals that had been years deferred: I lost weight and got in shape; I became tidier and better organized; I improved my relationships and my finances. Excited by my progress, I began to share my system with business colleagues, friends, and family who in turn passed the system on to others. My thriving test lab led me to a simple conclusion: *Microresolutions work*.

We live in the age of the small and powerful, where micro computer chips, tablets, iPods, smart phones, and their apps drive productivity at work and at home. Microfinancing is eliminating poverty one family at a time. Nanotechnology is revolutionizing medicine. Critical communications arrive in 140-character tweets, hitting global distribution lists in microseconds. These tools are targeted, designed to fill a specific need exactly and deliver value immediately. So it is with microresolutions—each is designed to hit a specific personal-improvement target exactly and deliver benefits immediately.

Our fast-paced, multitasking days are packed so full that the thought of adding one more to-do, meeting one more need, or pursuing one new personal objective can be overwhelming. Microresolutions slip easily into our crowded lives, quietly working their magic while we go on juggling schedules and meeting endless obligations. Indeed, microresolutions make it possible to achieve continuous self-improvement without breaking a sweat.

Microresolutions are fun and easy and take effect immediately. But before plunging into the mechanics of microresolutions—how and why they work—we should first ask ourselves, why do traditional resolutions so often end in defeat?

Why Resolutions Fail

We all know someone who transformed himself through an act of will—went from flabby to fit, from spendthrift to investor, from slob to house-proud neat freak. At one time or another, nearly all of us succeed in reaching some ambitious personal goal such as running the marathon or finishing a degree. But more familiar are the resolutions we make on New Year's Day and abandon in March, the midnight champagne a distant memory and our forsaken resolutions a lingering and dispiriting hangover. The broken New Year's resolution is a cultural staple, fodder for countless punch lines poking fun at the universal folly of self-improvement. We laugh along, in on the joke, yet the promises we make ourselves are serious, not silly. With so much on the line, why do we fail so often?

We Make the Wrong Resolutions

Google "New Year's resolutions" and you'll turn up dozens of links devoted to popular and worthwhile personal goals. Most of these are what I call *wannabe* resolutions: *I will be fit, I will be organized, I will be assertive.* These iconic resolutions are very much like wishes in disguise: *I wish I were buff, I wish I were on top of my game, I wish I weren't such a doormat.* These resolutions focus on *being*, not *doing*.

Years ago in drama class I learned from a master that *to act* means *to do*, not *to be*. Many young actors make the mistake of trying *to be* onstage, playing "I'm angry," "I'm sad," "I'm tough." But impersonating the qualities and emotions of a character—"I'm an angry tough guy with a heart of gold"— leaves these actors little *to do* onstage. In assuming a persona, they miss out on the real action of the drama, the process by which their character grows and becomes emotional. Great actors understand that the secret to behaving and feeling like a character is to focus on what the character *does*. They analyze how the character's explicit actions reveal his objectives, attitudes, and values. They concentrate on playing each action fully, and the sequence of actions adds up to an authentic characterization, a true experience, and an emotional response from themselves and from the audience. The acting lesson? *If you focus on doing what the character does, being the character will follow.**

The same lesson applies to the resolutions you make and hope to keep. If you resolve to *be organized*, you'll likely find yourself flashing a virtual BE ORGANIZED! sign in your head every time you pick up the mail or sit down at your desk. But browbeating yourself to "be organized" every moment of the day will soon exhaust your will to change. Like an actor onstage trying to impersonate *an angry tough guy*, your focus is in the wrong place. Rather than commanding yourself *to be* what you are not—an organized person—you must define explicit actions to practice, one by one, until you begin to do what an organized person does *automatically*.

Microresolutions focus on doing, not being. Being different follows, rather than precedes, deliberate action.

We Depend Solely on Willpower to Succeed

Wannabe resolutions are stimulated by powerful fantasies of a future self. Imagining ourselves happier, fitter, or more financially secure inspires us and ignites our will to change. If our goal is *to be slim and fit*, we visualize ourselves looking svelte on the beach come summer and stick a buff pinup on the fridge to bolster our resolve. Our dream self is so inspiring that we feel certain we can sustain our will no matter how demanding the regimen we adopt to reach our goal. But before opening day at the beach our will collapses, thwarted by the long-established behaviors that sustain our everyday lives. We chastise ourselves for our lack of self-control, but in fact our willpower was simply

---

* In his journal notes for the completion of his final, unfinished novel, *The Last Tycoon* (1941), F. Scott Fitzgerald wrote: "Action is character."

outmatched by the tenacity of our habits, attitudes, and routines.

We are each driven by a system of unconscious habits and preferences nurtured early in life and entrenched through repetition. These established behaviors and attitudes form a kind of *autopilot*, which quietly and efficiently manages most of the routine tasks and decision making that we perform each day, preserving precious mental energy and initiative for new learning, problem solving, and idea generation. We don't have to concentrate to tie our shoes—autopilot ties them for us. Autopilot makes the coffee, locks the door, and drives the car. But your autopilot may also skip the gym, binge on sweets, overspend, or snap at your spouse. Operating largely unnoticed, the deeply rooted habits of autopilot drive individual outcomes, both good and bad. New behavioral research confirms that we are neither aware of nor in control of the routines that govern our lives. As British researchers summarized in a recent study published in *Health Psychology*, "[habit] automaticity may be broken down into a number of features: lack of awareness, mental efficiency, lack of control and lack of conscious intent."* In other words, we don't think about what we're doing; we just do it, unaware of how our autopilot drives us toward success or failure.

When we decide to improve ourselves—to shake things up—we run straight into resistance from autopilot. While the autopilot system in a car can easily be switched off so that the driver can resume control, disabling any part of your personal autopilot requires real effort. Autopilot likes routine and resists change. The more change we impose on ourselves, the more resistance we must overcome. And yet we nearly always shoot

---

* S. Orbell and B. Verplanken, "The Automatic Component of Habit in Health Behavior: Habit as Cue-Contingent Automaticity," *Health Psychology* 29, no. 4 (July 2010): 374—83.

for an instant transformation, resolving *to be slim, to be neat, to be on time.* Such *wannabe* resolutions require changing scores of behaviors and put us broadly at war with autopilot. Resolving *to be slim* means changing your habits in almost every eating circumstance: what you eat, how often you eat, how much you eat, the way you eat. Suddenly every action, every choice demands scrutiny, conscious effort, and *willpower.*

In a seminal 2000 study on the dynamics of willpower, researchers Mark Muraven and Roy Baumeister demonstrated that self-control is a limited, physiological resource that is easily exhausted:

> We found that after an act of self-control, subsequent unrelated self-control operations suffer. . . . After resisting temptations, people perform more poorly on tests of vigilance and are less able to resist subsequent temptations.*

The more we draw on our willpower, the sooner it gives out. The broad resolutions we favor place unreasonable demands on our self-control. In order to muscle through a behavioral change, our willpower has to wrestle autopilot all day long—no wonder we cry uncle before we make it to the beach! Despite our determination to succeed, after a few weeks of valiant battle our willpower collapses, outmatched by the entrenched habits and preferences that quietly rule our lives.

The willpower-driven resolution is a top-down approach to self-improvement—we command ourselves to be different and try to force our behavior and attitudes into line. The microresolution

---

* M. Muraven and R. F. Baumeister, "Self-Regulation and Depletion of Limited Resources: Does Self-Control Resemble a Muscle?" *Psychological Bulletin* 126, no. 2 (2000): 247–59.

system is a bottom-up approach, focusing relentlessly on one or two significant behavioral changes until they are driven into autopilot, where they require no deliberate effort— willpower—to sustain. A ground-level perspective offers visibility for the long run; the top-down perspective—the bird's-eye view of the treetops, not the trees—obscures the path and seldom produces insights that lead to success the next time. But working from the ground up we can see in detail exactly what is in our way. By focusing closely on fundamental behaviors and attitudes, we increase our self-awareness and accelerate our progress.

A microresolution is designed to reform a precise autopilot activity and requires little willpower to succeed.

We're Too Impatient

The new year is a time of restless spirits. After so many holiday months filled with self-indulgence—eating more, drinking more, spending more, letting go—we're eager to jump on the wagon and reform ourselves straightaway. We seek out shortcuts and gimmicks that promise to speed our transformation, convinced there is some magic formula to make us what we *wannabe*. Fueling our impatience is the fear that if it takes us too long to achieve a goal, we will give up before we succeed. Our mindless rushing blurs our vision, and we fail to observe how quiet habits and hidden attitudes keep us from succeeding. The next time we try to self-improve, we make exactly the same mistakes.

Transformation is a process, not an event. (Even with the help of a fairy godmother, Cinderella ended up stranded on the road from the palace when her coach turned back into a pumpkin.) And why would you want to skip the process? Consciously nurturing change makes us smarter, more self-aware, and builds a powerful foundation for continued growth. Being able to re-peat our steps from A to B *is* the magic formula for making our achievements permanent.

The key to lasting transformation is not speed or force but nurture.

We Underestimate Our Mental and Emotional Resistance to Change

Familiar habits and behaviors sustain and comfort us in our daily lives. Our mental, emotional, and physical habits are closely tied to the family values and routines we learned in childhood. All that early conditioning—your parents pestering you to hang up your coat, chew with your mouth closed, clean your plate, and be a good sport—established behaviors and preferences that allow you to operate on autopilot with respect to many of the actions and decisions you make each day. Disturbing these routines cre-ates awkwardness, mental fatigue, emotional stress, and a strong impulse to revert to what feels *right*—to autopilot. The more change we take on, the more mental and emotional resistance we arouse in ourselves, such resistance brewing often just beneath the surface of our consciousness.

The intense focus of a microresolution helps expose our veiled mindset and the subtle interplay among habits, attitudes, and values that block progress. Like a scientific experiment that alters a single variable at a time in order to precisely observe cause and effect, the single-minded focus of a microresolution exposes the source of our resistance to change. Once identified, a negative mindset can be addressed, undone, even turned in support of our objectives.

Microresolutions foster self-awareness and expose the hidden attitudes that thwart success.

We Expect to Fail

Sadly, having bailed on so many self-improvement missions, we've come to anticipate the inevitable moment when our will to change collapses and we revert to the comfort of our previous routines. The ghosts of failures past haunt each new endeavor, making it harder for us to believe in our ability to sustain progress and influence outcomes. As our willpower wanes, we are oddly consoled by the familiar sensation of giving up and giving way. *Yes, let's have that milkshake.*

The way to free ourselves from cynicism and reverse our expectation of failure is to learn how to make resolutions we can sustain.

A microresolution is easy to keep.

It was only after discovering the microresolution that I began to understand why so many of the pledges we make faithfully each year fail over time. Desperate and frustrated in the wake of one such disappointment, I made my first microresolution and thereby stumbled onto a system for making resolutions that succeed on the first try and are sustainable for a lifetime. But I don't want to get ahead of myself—as I said, it all started with a broken New Year's resolution.

My First Microresolution

New Year's Day. Resolution time again. What did I resolve last year? Oh, yes, I remember—to lose weight and exercise more. How did that turn out? *Let's see . . . do the math . . . wait for it . . .* a net gain of three pounds one year later.

It wasn't hard to remember my resolution or the one from the year before. Like that hopeless self-reformer Bridget Jones, who begins her eponymous diary with a list of New Year's resolutions that includes "Losing three inches from thighs," only to acknowledge her failure by March 21 with the entry, "Right: for coming year will reactivate New Year's Resolutions,"* my weight-loss pledge had become perennial. On this New Year's I still needed to lose ten pounds, but I shrank from renewing my pledge, because I couldn't face failing at it again. *No point in wasting yet another precious New Year's resolution on that intractable ten pounds*, I reasoned. I had other self-improvement goals to pursue and I wanted to make a resolution I was sure I could keep—that is, one that didn't require eating less or going to the gym. So I picked a new category of self-improvement and resolved:

To be organized

My resolution seemed straightforward and achievable, much easier than losing weight. I was energized and determined to succeed. I went out and bought organizers for my desk at home, with slots for bills pending and bills paid, items to file and items to read (not surprisingly, container and organizer stores do their biggest business just after the New Year). I created new files with color-coded labels, cleaned up my work space, and caught up on old business. But soon the organizer slots were overflowing and my work area piled up again. I felt weary every time I looked at my desk. After three months of trying, I had failed.

I was so horrified to realize that I had failed at my *easy* resolution that I refused to concede complete defeat. If I couldn't achieve *be organized* in three months, what could I achieve that

---

* Helen Fielding, *Bridget Jones's Diary* (Penguin Books, 1996).

would make a difference? *To be organized* was, finally, an abstract goal. What was one concrete and specific action I could take that would make me *more* organized in a meaningful way?

I examined all the ways in which I was disorganized that caused me stress. One issue was that I couldn't always find notes when I needed them. For most of my life I had been able to rely on my memory alone, recalling discussions, research, important details, upcoming meetings, and to-do lists with near-total accuracy. As I approached forty, I needed to supplement my memory with notes, but I wasn't systematic—my note taking was sporadic and incomplete. At home and at work, I had multiple notebooks of varying sizes that I would randomly grab when I needed to write something down. Often, I would write my notes and follow-ups directly on the agenda or presentation for a meeting. I collected notes throughout the day, with some ending up in my handbag, some on my desk at work, some on my desk at home. I lost valuable time hunting for meeting notes, an important phone number, a reference. I decided to focus my resolution solely on this single organizational issue. I resolved:

To put all my notes in one notebook

I bought a small, serious-looking journal to capture my notes. I was determined to succeed and break the curse of the failed New Year's resolution and considered my new resolution so modest that it would be a snap to keep. I was wrong. Because my habit was to depend on my memory, I didn't automatically reach for my notebook before meetings or phone calls; I just plunged in. Once I realized I didn't have my notebook in front of me, I didn't want to break the flow of conversation to fish it out of my bag because I preferred to give myself to the dynamism of the moment. I'd sit down at my desk to take a phone call and realize that my notebook was on a table across the room. With paper right in front of me, did I really need to trot around my desk and retrieve it? A team member would grab me with a request as I was heading out the door in a hurry—wouldn't I just remember all the details without stopping to make notes? I found my resolution both boring and irritating to keep.

But because my resolution was obviously feasible, I felt tremendous pressure to succeed. Because my resolution was reasonable, I couldn't throw up my hands and say, "This is just too hard. The timing is bad. I'll try again in a few months." Because my resolution was specific, success was easy to measure—every time I ignored the notebook rule I could see my failure immediately and correct myself. Because my resolution was limited, I wasn't overwhelmed and was able to dedicate focus and willpower to achieving my goal. The modesty of my resolution also forced me to face the fact that if I couldn't follow through with one very reasonable change in behavior, then my hopes for greater self-improvement were simply fantasies.

I stuck with it. I forced myself to put all my notes in my little red book. If I had an idea for a client, I wrote it in the book. Confirmation numbers—in the book. Recommended articles, Web sites, events—in the book. Random contacts I might never need again—in the book. Packing list—in the book. Priorities and to-do lists—in the book. Bullet points for my next presentation—in the book. Recipe from a friend—in the book. After weeks of reminding myself to use the notebook, I noticed my feelings of resistance and awkwardness fading as the notebook became second nature—I just did it without thinking, like brushing my teeth. As soon as I sat down in a meeting or at my desk, I reached for the notebook. Now I could locate what I needed almost immediately, without stress or drama. Notes I once would have deemed throwaways proved significant weeks on. The notebook rule that I had at first found intrusive and constraining I now experienced as empowering and liberating. My stress level declined. *I had become more organized.*

Moreover, I had succeeded in keeping a resolution, building a good habit, and improving my life. Unlike the resolution *to be organized*, where I could have declared success only after sustaining multiple behavioral changes over time to reach some ideal definition of *organized*, my notebook resolution brought me an immediate and obvious benefit, as specific and concrete as the resolution itself: All my notes ended up in one place. Succeeding at my resolution and experiencing its rewards energized me, and I lost my sense of helplessness.

Now I reexamined my initial resolution—*to be organized*—and understood better why it hadn't succeeded. I had made a project of it—a big, one-off project—to clean my desk, catch up, and reorganize my files. I had had a burst of organizational zeal that resulted in some progress, similar to going on a crash diet. But I had failed to develop systematic behaviors—habits—to maintain my organizational gains over time. I had tried to supersede my ingrained and unconscious behaviors and attitudes by willing myself to be organized without really asking myself what exactly I needed to do differently—*forever*—to succeed. The notebook resolution worked because I had focused exclusively on a single area of disorganization until I had formed a new habit and mindset that allowed me to sustain my new behavior without mental energy. My relentless focus on the notebook habit had driven it into autopilot.

Experiencing my resistance to the notebook rule exposed aspects of my mindset that had never been clear to me before. For the first time I realized that I had unconsciously associated strict administrative systems with dull bureaucracy, at odds with dynamism, creativity, and the naturally logical and organized mind. It didn't feel right to me that something as humdrum as note taking should require tenacity and energy. Experiencing the benefits of my new habit caused me to place a higher value on systematic behavior and upgraded my organizational instincts. As a result of my reformed mindset, some of my other organizational behaviors began to improve spontaneously.

Inspired by my success, I decided to revisit the challenge of losing weight and see if I could successfully apply the lessons I had learned from my notebook resolution. What if, instead of resolving *to be thin by summer*, I examined my eating habits and targeted one specific behavioral change that would be achievable and impactful?

At that time I was working at a Wall Street firm that offered abundant snacks in conference-room settings. During meetings we passed around china plates lined with doilies and piled high with brownies, blondies, oatmeal and chocolate chip cookies. Eating just one of these rich treats produced a sugar high powerful enough to outlast the longest meeting. But it was hard to eat just one. Sometimes I would eat two (or three), and each cookie was probably 350 calories. I often left the conference room in a food coma, overfull and facing a sugar crash later in the day. I resolved:

Never to eat a conference-room cookie again

I didn't resolve *never to eat a cookie again* or *never to snack again* or *never to eat food in a conference room again*. Instead, I kept my resolution *reasonable* and *limited* and resolved only to forswear the ubiquitous and addictive conference-room cookies. Because my resolution was specific, success was easy to measure: I was in the conference room; the cookies were passed; if I passed on the cookies, I had succeeded. It was hard the first few times the plate came my way; over time it became automatic. I was glad not to leave the meeting feeling terrible about myself and mildly sick to my stomach. Eating the cookies in the conference room had been a habit, something I anticipated every time I entered a meeting. My targeted resolution broke that bad habit forever. I never ate a conference-room cookie again, and my resolution arrested the slow but steady upward climb of my weight (actually losing weight required more microresolutions, as we shall see).

Experiencing the power and benefits of microresolutions taught me that significant and permanent behavioral change can be achieved with intense, targeted focus; that targeted focus leads to valuable and actionable personal insights; that limited resolutions can produce immediate and sustainable benefits; and that succeeding at a reasonable resolution daily is more trans-forming than failing at an unrealistic resolution annually.

As my understanding of the dynamics of microresolutions grew with experience, I learned how to identify the best resolu-tions, frame them, tune them, and keep them. I established rules and strategies for making successful microresolutions that are detailed in the next chapters. Most important, I learned that to sustain progress over time, a resolution must create habits that become part of personal autopilot.

Habits Rule

> Powerful indeed is the empire of habit.
>
> —Publilius Syrus, 42 BC

Habits. Groan. Sounds dull and boring, doesn't it? Habits are, well, routine. And the part that isn't routine is negative, as in, "I have a bad habit of biting my nails." But a habit is any behavior or attitude you practice without conscious decision, and that's just about everything. Yes, habits are routine, but they are anything but boring.

Each of us has a unique system of habits nurtured over a lifetime. What you do by habit takes very little mental energy. If you brush your teeth every morning, you do it without thinking, and if you don't do it, you don't feel right. The routines we learned in childhood support us throughout our lives, for better or for worse. It's work to unmake a habit—healthy or unhealthy—once it's part of a routine. Writing in a recent issue of the *Journal of Experimental Social Psychology*, researchers Wendy Wood and David Neal defined habits simply as "psychological dispositions to repeat past behavior."* Repeating and perfecting behavior is efficient—mindlessly performing routines conserves critical mental energy for initiative and decision making.

The habits learned in childhood require little or no mental energy to maintain. A very neat person likely learned the dozens of behaviors that we think of as *neat* in childhood, each desired behavior drilled relentlessly until it became a matter of unconscious habit. Thus, aspiring *to be neat* means doing the work of childhood—drilling one *neat* habit at a time until it takes permanent hold. Yet most of us stay stuck in our *wannabe* fantasies, discounting the effort required to build even a single habit—such as making the bed every day—to advance our goal.

For those who grew up making the bed every morning, bed making is as simple as breathing; the minute they're out of bed, they make it. Years of repetition have fostered such efficiency and skill that the bed practically makes itself. But if you did not

---

* D. T. Neal et al., "How Do Habits Guide Behavior? Perceived and Actual Triggers of Habits in Daily Life," *Journal of Experimental Social Psychology* 48, no. 2 (March 2012).

grow up with this habit, acquiring it takes some effort. You might feel oppressed from the moment you even start to think about making the bed. It's a dull task. It takes too much time. It doesn't come out looking nice. You're already late for work. But if you've signed up to a microresolution *to make the bed each morning before breakfast*, you'll figure out how to get it done, because it's absolutely doable, unlike a resolution *to keep the house neat all the time*. You'll get better at it every day, so that it takes less time and comes out looking better. You'll become expert at cornering sheets and plumping pillows simply by doing it over and over. Finally, after making your bed every morning for a couple of months, you won't be able to stand the sight of it unmade. This is how habits are formed, standards raised, and progress achieved.

In addition to demonstrating and drilling behavior patterns, childhood authority figures also instill in us a *mindset* of values, attitudes, and preferences that constantly reinforce those patterns. Thus does our very character get tied up with our habits, making even a small change in routine stressful. Improving oneself by altering any long-standing behavior pattern is a breakthrough, a liberating experience that leads to personal insight and an appetite for greater personal growth.

Habits also serve as experiential paradigms for minting similar habits more quickly. For example, if you are generally late and you resolve to be on time for a weekly event, say, an exercise class, once you nail being on time for that class, your on-time experience will change your mindset and provide a model for improving your punctuality in other areas. Thus, a successful microresolution is like laying a behavioral cornerstone to support dozens of good habits to follow. Some of these new habits will be the result of conscious effort, but others will emerge spontaneously in response to the fresh perspective and revitalized mindset that come from new experience and the rewards from making a single change in personal behavior.

What gives habits their lasting power is that they are automatic, mindless. Thus, to change ourselves we must cultivate autopilot's opposite—mindfulness. The more aware we are of the habits that manage our lives, the more control we have over our future. Habits aren't boring; they are the very stuff we're made of—just ask Western civilization's most celebrated philosopher:

> We are what we repeatedly do. Excellence, then, is not
> an act but a habit.
>
> —Aristotle

And what is self-improvement but the search for excellence? Let's begin.

PART 1

THE SEVEN RULES OF MICRORESOLUTIONS

CHAPTER 1

How to Make a Microresolution

Are you ready to make a microresolution?

Start by asking yourself what you'd like to improve about your life. Sticking with the example we explored in the last chapter, the first expression of your goal might be framed in broad terms—"I'd like to be neat"—and that's a reasonable place to start. Yet *neat* is not a state you can adopt; rather, it's a set of distinct behaviors that add up to *neat* according to *your* definition—there's neat and then there's *neat*. Every personal-improvement goal within your power can be reduced to a list of behaviors, whether your ultimate objective is to be neat, lose weight, get fit, be nicer to your spouse, become organized, be on time, save money, advance your career, or get more sleep.

So taking *neat* as our example, the first step is to deconstruct what you mean by *neat*. Your most pressing neatness issues might be to keep clothes hung up and to stay on top of laundry; or perhaps every drawer is crammed and the bed never gets made; or maybe you leave dishes overnight and let items pile up on surfaces. Don't bother compiling an exhaustive list; just pinpoint one or two behavioral changes you think would make a difference. Remember, you're not trying to solve for *neat* overall; you're just looking to identify a discrete behavioral change that will move the neat dial in the right direction.

If your neatness target is focused on managing clutter, your first resolution might be as simple as resolving to allow only certain items on certain surfaces. It's hard to keep a surface organized when it's littered with items that have nothing to do with its utility—*e.g.*, coins and a comb and keys on a desk; magazines and bills on a bureau; mail stacked up on a kitchen island. If every surface you have is just a parking lot for *whatever*, dedicating surfaces might be a good first resolution (you might even want to start with just one surface). Once items are segregated in logical groups it's much easier to see what's required to keep a particular surface orderly.

For example, if your desk is overflowing with piles of un-opened and unsorted mail, making a microresolution to sort and discard mail before you place it on your desk will probably eliminate three-quarters of your pileup (neatness) and allow you to see at a glance what really needs handling (organization). If clothes sit in a heap on the bedroom chair all week, resulting in a mind-numbing weekend session of hanging up (now very wrinkled) clothing, you might consider a resolution to hang up your clothes as soon as you take them off or start with a resolution allowing any set of clothes only twenty-four hours on the chair.

Mindset Messaging

What about the mental habits that keep you from succeeding in your goals? In the present case, how might you improve your neatness *mindset*—values, preferences, and attitudes—to advance your objective? For example, a neat mindset might include the attitude *it's more productive to work at a clean desk*. Such an attitude can be taught through practice, just as one can teach oneself a physical behavior through repetition. You can do this by resolving to give yourself a *microresolution message* designed to improve your governing mindset. A change in mindset will drive behavioral change, just as a successful behavioral change ultimately alters your mindset through experience. As the nineteenth-century psychologist and pragmatist William James observed, "The greatest revelation of our generation is the discovery that human beings, by changing the inner attitudes of their minds, can change the outer aspects of their lives."

The mechanism for changing your mindset through messaging is the same as for changing a physical behavior: a targeted and limited resolution practiced relentlessly until it becomes automatic. The success of a microresolution message is measured solely by your remembering to give yourself the message in the circumstance you've selected, and that's it. It's like a mental tweet synchronized to a specific trigger.

For example, someone working on *neat* might resolve to send himself the message *It's really just as fast to hang it up* when removing his coat. Using the removal of the coat to *cue* the message will disrupt the autopilot attitude *I don't have time to hang it up right now* and likely lead, over time, to a preference for hanging up the coat. To once again quote James, "The mere thought of a behavior tends to lead to the performance of it," or as Sigmund Freud put it, "The thought is father to the deed."

Some of my most successful microresolutions have been mindset targeted. I once resolved to send myself the following message when I was tempted to snack in the late afternoon: *I enjoy dinner so much more when I'm hungry for it.* My resolution didn't prohibit an afternoon snack; it simply posited the greater pleasure of sitting down to dinner with good appetite.

Repeating this message to myself when I was tempted by a treat in the late afternoon led me to manage my snacks more closely and to give up noshing while preparing dinner (you know, that little piece of French bread, that extra glass of wine) and did indeed result in deeper enjoyment of the family meal I prepared each night. Repeating this message ultimately changed my mindset; I realized that by *choosing* to snack richly I was *choosing* to enjoy dinner less. I began selecting lighter snacks and timing them to result in greater appetite. Never before had I "saved" my appetite; I had always been an indiscriminate snacker. So much so, in fact, that every diet plan I had ever drawn up for myself had been focused on how many calories I could carve out for my snack allowance. Today I so prefer to save my appetite for meals that I seldom snack at all, and it's all due to the mindset shift created by faithfully repeating my *hungry for dinner* message when tempted by treats in the afternoon.

Living on the Edge

Microresolutions helped me to discover that the real action in self-improvement happens around the edges, at what we might call *the vital margin*. Drastic actions that try to get at the red-hot core of behavioral change (such as crash diets) nearly always end in failure, but a discrete and meaningful shift in behavior will always succeed if given enough focus. A single change in eating habits can result in permanent weight loss; a shift in a spending pattern can yield substantial savings; a subtle change in communication can enhance a relationship; a change in attitude can create new opportunities on the job. To prove this you need only see that the reverse is true: A small but negative shift in behavior will take you further from your goals. Although you may not realize it in real time, a slight change in habit can cause you to gain weight, take on debt, poison a relationship, or hold you back at work. It turns out that the marginal is, *in practice*, the very epicenter of behavioral change. Making a microresolution is about applying yourself with single-minded purpose to an action at the margin that will propel you forward and make a positive difference in your life. In self-improvement, it's working the margin that gives you the edge.

So this is the work: Identify a discrete change in behavior that will make a difference, and drill that behavior with single-minded purpose until it becomes second nature. The chapters that follow are devoted to teaching you how to use microresolutions to target and effect a change in habit at the vital margin. If you stick to the microresolution rules, you'll be able to make instant progress in any self-improvement category, from weight loss to achieving a more loving relationship. The more you succeed, the more you'll understand yourself and the smarter your next microresolution will be. A microresolution is a self-improvement adventure that pays off—every time.

CHAPTER 2

Don't Make Resolutions You Can't Keep

Your microresolution must be a pledge you are sure you have the power to keep—a *no excuses* resolution. To be absolutely achievable, it must be limited. Resolutions to *walk everywhere all the time* or *never eat sweets again* or *give up online shopping* don't qualify. Put aside that familiar temptation to try to fix everything all at once by tomorrow and focus instead on making a resolution that is so reasonable you are sure you can make it stick. Your microresolution should target a limited behavioral change that is reasonable enough that you can force yourself to keep it—don't overreach.

Rule 1: A Microresolution Is Easy

Let's take a common resolution, *to get in shape*, and define a fitness micro that is limited, achievable, and impactful—easy. Let's say you'd like to increase your fitness by walking to work once a week. Your resolution could be to walk the entire way (thirty minutes), to get off the bus or train two stops sooner (fifteen minutes), or to park farther away (ten minutes)—whatever your circumstances, just start with the resolution you are sure you can keep. If you're sedentary and your settled routine is to ride to work, suddenly resolving to walk every day wouldn't be reasonable. Once you begin your walking resolution, you're going to discover internal and external obstacles that you must resolve to make it work. Overcommitting at the outset to walk all five days just multiplies the obstacles you'll need to overcome each week in order to succeed.

The weather, your mood, your energy level, additional clothing demands, the growing boredom of your route, and the pressure of your schedule will present themselves as reasons for not following through on your five-day pledge. You'll begin to bargain with yourself over the scope of your commitment, renegotiating your resolution on a daily basis. Maybe walking five days is too much; how about three days? Maybe you weren't able to walk today, but how about tomorrow? If tomorrow is as good as today, why not the day after tomorrow? If any day is as good as today, pretty soon you will find yourself at the weekend wondering how it was that you didn't manage to walk a single day. It is by this kind of mental calculus that most traditional resolutions devolve and finally expire. Constant mental renegotiation—not today but tomorrow, not this week but next (*I'll gladly pay you Tuesday for a hamburger today*)—puts you in debt to your resolution until at last you are hopelessly behind in your commitment. Your shifting resolution loses all credibility as a priority, and soon you slip back into your old routines.

Repeatedly pressing the snooze button on your commitment turns out to be more than just demoralizing. Choosing to defer or renegotiate your resolution is *decision making*, and it turns out that decision making is a very expensive psychological activity. A 2007 willpower study conducted by Kathleen Vohs and Roy

Baumeister found that making decisions taxes the same limited mental resource as exercising self-control. The more decisions we have to make, the weaker our resolve becomes, a phenomenon the two researchers dubbed "decision fatigue."[*]

Vohs and Baumeister conducted several experiments in which participants were required to make a series of choices and were then tested for remaining levels of self-control. In one of these experiments, participating university students designated "Group 1" arrived at the test site and were each given a series of class choices to make from the university course catalog and a response sheet on which to formally record their selections. Subjects designated "Group 2" were instructed to familiarize themselves with the course catalog but weren't asked to make choices or given a response sheet. Each participant spent eight minutes on his assigned catalog activity and was then told that he would next take a math test predictive of success in the real world. Each participant was given a packet of study material, advised that fifteen minutes of study had been shown to increase the test score, and then left to study for fifteen minutes in a room that included magazines and video games. Participants were allowed to read the magazines and play the video games if they finished preparing before the study period had elapsed.

The researchers found that the students in Group 1, who had undergone the decision-making activity, "spent more time playing video games, reading magazines, and doing nothing than did non-depleted participants." Considering this and other similar experiments, the researchers concluded:

---

[*] Kathleen D. Vohs et al., "Making Choices Impairs Subsequent Self-Control: A Limited-Resource Account of Decision Making, Self-Regulation, and Active Initiative," *Journal of Personality and Social Psychology* 94, no. 5 (May 2008): 883–98.

> The present findings suggest that self-regulation, ac-
> tive initiative, and effortful choosing draw on the same
> psychological resource. Making decisions depletes that
> resource, thereby weakening the subsequent capacity
> for self-control and active initiative.*

In other words, the more decision making your resolution requires, the less resolve you'll actually have left to follow through, because decision making and self-control draw on the same limited mental resource. Making unrealistic commitments inevitably leads to frequent decisions about trade-offs, deferrals, and makeup sessions that deplete precious self-control reserves. Decisions are constantly required in carrying out a classic *wannabe* resolution such as *I resolve to be organized*. If you're disorganized and then suddenly command yourself to "be organized," every activity you engage in will require you to decide on the best, most organized approach, how to carry out the approach, how organized is organized enough, etc. Each time you stop yourself and ask, *Okay, what should I be doing here to be better organized?* you're engaging in decision making and depleting the limited resource of "self-regulation, active initiative, and effortful choosing" defined by Vohs and Baumeister and accelerating toward the moment when you just give up. *Small Move, Big Change* is focused on building behaviors that run on autopilot, where decision making is rarely involved.

The more challenging your resolution, the more likely that you will bargain yourself out of it altogether. The more feasible your commitment, the less tempted you'll be to talk yourself out of it and the more self-control you will conserve for actually performing the action of your resolution. Limit your

---

* Vohs et al., "Making Choices Impairs Subsequent Self-Control."

commitment to what you are sure you can accomplish—there is no partial credit for (or value in) a half-completed microresolution.

An easy microresolution would be to walk to work one day a week. Walking one day is reasonable, achievable, and a significant step toward becoming fitter and building the habit of walking. Besides, what you believe is easy will be harder than you think. Any change to established routine takes focus to achieve. You may still be tempted to ignore or defer your resolution, but because it's limited and reasonable (just one day) you'll be highly motivated to manage obstacles out of your way. Part of the magic of a microresolution is that you end up looking for solutions, not excuses. Because if you can't stare down one very reasonable self-improvement resolution, you'll have to face the fact that only a miracle or fateful cosmic jolt can alter the way you live every day.

But isn't it a smarter strategy, you might ask, *to resolve to walk five days a week and let it slip to two days rather than succeeding on just a single day?* You mean, trick yourself into a two-day commitment by failing at a five-day one? Absolutely not! Your most important goal is to learn how to make realistic commitments you can keep, so you can hold yourself accountable and count on progress every time you make a resolution. Don't try to fake yourself out; just set an expectation you can meet.

A resolution to walk one day a week doesn't mean you can't walk more than once. A microresolution doesn't limit what you want to do, only what you commit to do. If you're enjoying your once-a-week walk and you decide you want to walk more often, go ahead and walk more; just don't expand your resolution to more days until your one-day walk is an established habit.

The benefits of sticking with your microresolution will be anything but limited. Small changes bring big benefits. If you keep your resolution to walk to work once a week, you'll be fitter, arrive with a clearer head, rev your metabolism for the day, burn some calories, refresh your perspective with the change of seasons, and maybe find you enjoy it so much that you become an avid walker. You'll experience the satisfaction and empowerment that come from targeting an action, following through, and building a positive new habit. Experiencing success builds confidence and motivation and lifts the jinx of repeat defeats. Instead of anticipating failure, you'll learn to expect success, and the cycle of making, forsaking, and remaking resolutions will be broken forever.

Keep your resolution limited, reasonable, and achievable— *easy*.

CHAPTER 3

Doing It

A microresolution is an action: not something you commit to be but something you commit to do. A microresolution is not a wish, a philosophy, or a result; its straightforward purpose is to build, change, or eliminate a specific behavior or attitude. The action of your resolution is something you resolve to do or not to do or a message you resolve to give yourself in a given circumstance.

Rule 2: A Microresolution Is an Explicit and Measurable Action

Your microresolution must be explicit so there's no guessing about what to do, when to do it, or how to carry it out. Resolutions such as *I will exercise more* or *I will snack less* are worthless. Exercise more than what? Snack less than what? Resolving not to be defensive when you get feedback at work? You'll need to think about the specific circumstances under which you become defensive, the form your defensiveness takes, and what explicit message you can send yourself that will stop you from justifying yourself with your first breath. Pledging to do something twice a week? Which days? What time? Is online shopping eating up your time and your wallet? Take a look at how your present behavior leads you into unwanted purchases and zero in on a specific change in habit that could save you money, such as establishing a "no shopping" period during the hours you're most vulnerable to mindless browsing and impulse buying because your self-control has already been depleted by a day of initiative, decision making, and exercise of willpower.

The more explicit your resolution, the easier it will be to measure success, identify obstacles, and fine-tune your commitment for greater effectiveness. For example, if you resolve to handle personal administrative work once a week without specifying the day, you won't be able to measure your success until the week has ended, and all week long your undone resolution will loom over you, portending failure. And if you do fail to make time for your session, it will be difficult to see exactly what went wrong, since *any* day might have been *the* day. If your resolution requires a schedule, don't keep yourself guessing, *Will I or won't I today?* Settle on a day and time and stick to it. It's not until you get specific about *when* that you can get a handle on your own resistance to change or observe other obstacles that need to be addressed.

Explicit commitments do not constrain; to the contrary, they create certainty and comfort. Flexible or fuzzy resolutions, escape clauses, and loopholes result in stress, not greater freedom. Returning to the "walk to work" example discussed in rule 1, a commitment to walk on Monday mornings establishes a clear benchmark, freeing you from anxiety-provoking decisions and deferrals. Likewise, if you resolve to take care of personal administrative work on Wednesday nights, when you see items collecting in the in-basket, you won't worry about losing track because you'll *know* you're going to take care of it on Wednesday. Your initial scheduling may require some fine-tuning (see chapter 9, "Test-Driving Your Resolution"), but ultimately you need to establish a schedule you can stick with nearly all the time, or you'll just make it up as you go along, swapping and skipping days until you lose faith in yourself entirely.

Your resolution must focus on a specific change in behavior, not a result that can be achieved in multiple ways. For example, if you eat a two-hundred-calorie candy bar every afternoon as a snack, you might make a microresolution to eat half a candy bar, substitute a less caloric (and perhaps healthier) treat, or eliminate that particular snack from your diet altogether. The focus is on performing a specific action, and success is measured solely by whether or not you follow through with that action every day until it becomes established behavior.

Compare that approach with a resolution *to eliminate one hundred calories a day*. You might think such a resolution passes muster because one hundred calories is precise and measurable. But it's not a specific and measurable action, so it fails the test. There are many actions you could take to eliminate one hundred calories, and you might make a different choice—take a different action—on any given day. The only way to measure success is to wait until you have consumed and totaled your last calorie of the day and see if the hundred-calorie reduction has been met. A microresolution to cut a habitual afternoon snack of a candy bar in half is an explicit and measurable action; a pledge to eliminate one hundred calories daily is a math problem that must be solved every day (decisions, decisions).

A resolution *to get a good night's sleep* is a worthy goal but a total floozy of a commitment in microresolution terms. A good night's sleep is a result, not an action. How do you define a good night's sleep, and what keeps you from getting one now? What's

17

an action you can take that will increase your chances of getting a better night's sleep? For example, a resolution *to get ready for bed at 9:00 p.m. on nights at home* is a specific action that will clear the path to a good night's sleep by making sure that by the time you feel totally wiped you'll be able to head to bed immediately. Be absolutely specific in laying out the action of your resolution—what, when, how.

Cuing Your Resolution

Once you've carefully defined the action of your resolution, you'll need to establish a context for your new behavior by linking it to a time, activity, or situation. Habits are triggered by specific *cues*: saying "thank you" (habit) when served (cue); brushing teeth (habit) at bedtime (cue); saying "I told you so" (habit) when proved right (cue); serving yourself seconds (habit) when your plate is empty (cue); reading e-mail immediately (habit) when sitting down at the computer (cue). A strong link between cue and behavior creates a habit with lasting power.

Our responses to cues generally follow an unconscious pattern created over time through repetition. In a 2010 study on habit automaticity published in the journal *Health Psychology*, researchers Sheina Orbell and Bas Verplanken explained how actions once guided by *need* can result in a lasting cue:response linking (i.e., *autopilot*) divorced from any conscious goal:

> [A] person's initial decision to eat a cookie when drinking a cup of tea might be guided by an active goal state (e.g., feeling hungry). However, over time the goal becomes less necessary as cookie eating is repeated and becomes integrated with the act of

drinking tea so that it can be triggered by the cue alone.*

In the same study, the research team established that cues could also be deliberately created. In one experiment, each subject was given a packet of dental floss, educated on the benefits of flossing, and asked to fill out a questionnaire regarding their intention to floss. Half the subjects were given a questionnaire that concluded with the following statement:

> You are more likely to carry out your intention to perform dental flossing every day if you make a decision about when and where. Most people perform dental flossing in the bathroom immediately after they brush their teeth at night. Others prefer to do it in the morning after breakfast. Write down where and when you intend to floss your teeth every day for the next 4 weeks.

Other than this statement and the space to write down when and where to floss, the questionnaire given to both groups of study subjects was identical.

At the conclusion of the study the researchers assessed the flossing habits of both groups and found that the subjects in the group that had received the "statement" questionnaire were far more likely to have flossed regularly than those subjects who received the "basic" questionnaire. The researchers concluded that those subjects who were required by their questionnaires to specify when and where they intended to floss flossed more regularly

---

* S. Orbell and B. Verplanken, "The Automatic Component of Habit in Health Behavior: Habit as Cue-Contingent Automaticity," *Health Psychology* 29, no. 4 (July 2010): 374–83.

because they had first consciously identified a context, or *cue*, to trigger their new behavior.

Specifying a cue is part of making your microresolution explicit. The cue you establish can be calendar based (walk to work on Monday mornings) or contextual. In searching for a contextual cue, often the best strategy is to use an existing habit to trigger the new behavior. In the study cited above, one group received instructions suggesting they floss after nightly tooth brushing or after breakfast, thus creating a link between the new behavior (flossing) and an existing habit (nightly tooth brushing or eating breakfast). By linking the action of your resolution to one of your existing habits, you can speed the movement of your new behavior into autopilot.

For example, I once had to identify a cue for checking my priority list several times a day at work. Although I kept a priority list in my notebook, I was often sidetracked by phone calls, e-mails, meetings, and impromptu discussions and decisions. Hours would fly by before I remembered to review the list I had brought to work with me. By the end of the day I had accomplished a lot and cleared roadblocks for others but hadn't always attended to what was most important for me to get done. This often resulted in a late night or, if I lost track for too long, a significant delay in following through. I searched for an existing habit to act as a reminder to keep in closer contact with my list.

I resolved:

To review my priority list before checking e-mail at my desk throughout the day

I tied the action of my resolution (*review my priority list*) to an existing habit (*reading e-mail at my desk*), thereby ensuring I would be cued several times a day to review my priority list.

Reviewing my priorities before reading e-mail helped me to achieve a better balance between managing ongoing tactical needs and advancing strategic priorities. Note that my resolution required me only to review priorities when reading e-mail *at my desk*, exempting the quick intraday smart-phone checks required to operate efficiently in my job. I had solved the problem of keeping all my priorities in one place when I established the notebook habit with my first microresolution; now I built upon that solid habit with a new resolution that increased my organization and effectiveness.

Microresolution messages often require carefully defined cues. One very successful resolution I made was the microresolution message I used as a hypothetical example in chapter 1: sending myself the message *It's really just as fast to hang it up* when I slipped off my coat in the evening. Establishing an explicit cue for the message—the removal of my coat when I came home—made it possible to measure how successful I was in remembering to give myself the message. As soon as my coat would slip from my shoulders, the message would pop into my head. Day after day, the cue firing off the message kept me from dropping my coat in a chair and, over time, undid my bad habit of leaving clothes on the bedroom chair, because I came to *believe* that *it's really just as fast to hang it up*.

A resolution focused on eliminating a negative personal behavior is often cued by an impulse that arises internally, as in the case of Janet, who wanted to eliminate a certain curse word from her vocabulary. Janet made a microresolution to substitute the word *boring* every time she was tempted to use the nastier word. In Janet's case, the cue was the *impulse* to say the offensive word—the cue was, so to speak, right on the tip of her tongue.

The specificity of your microresolution and its cue makes it possible to measure your success with accuracy, pinpoint the nature of any resistance to change, and tune your resolution for maximum effectiveness. Make your commitment only when you have made your resolution explicit—what you're going to do, when you're going to do it, and how it will be cued.

CHAPTER 4

Instant Gratification

A microresolution's time frame is today, not someday. A microresolution's payoff is immediate, obvious, and sustainable forever. Unlike *wannabe* resolutions, where rewards are promised sometime in the future, each microresolution carries its own payload—what you pledge to do is what you get, as long as you follow through.

Rule 3: A Microresolution Pays Off Up Front

A microresolution *to make the bed each morning before breakfast* achieves its goal and delivers its benefit as soon and as long as the resolution is kept. By contrast, a resolution *to keep the house neat all the time*—made by a person who leaves dishes in the sink, lets surfaces pile up, and has overflowing laundry, a messy desk, and a bed that never gets made—has very little chance of succeeding, as neatness is a function of numerous habits and a mindset that can't be realized instantaneously. So the benefits of *keep the house neat* are projected into the future, to the *someday* when *keep the house neat* is finally achieved. But a microresolution *to make the bed each morning before breakfast* is achievable today and its benefit immediate—a made bed, a neater room, a more relaxing bedtime, perhaps a better sleep. The pristine bed may inspire more general tidiness in the bedroom, but the microresolution's exclusive target is *the bed*.

A microresolution to give up saying "I told you so" benefits your relationship the very first time you stop yourself from saying it, unlike the generalized resolution *to get along better with my partner*, where the strategy is unfixed and the measurement of success subjective. In trying *to get along better with my partner*, there may be better and worse days, but there won't be any way to relate the ups and downs to any specific change in behavior. However, if you know that saying "I told you so" to your partner creates friction, then it follows that when you stop saying it in all its forms, that friction will vanish. It won't mean that all your relationship issues are solved, but it will mean that you're refraining from scoring points at your partner's expense, and that, all on its own, has real value. Likewise, if you pledge to end your biweekly one-on-one meeting with your boss by asking for feedback, you'll instantly give your superior a more favorable impression of your maturity and professionalism, build trust, encourage dialogue, and give yourself a chance to benefit from your superior's perspective.

A New Year's resolution to *lose twenty pounds by summer* may find you recalculating every week how you might still be able to reach your goal despite the fact that your progress has plateaued, but a microresolution to *stop eating after 8:00 p.m.* delivers a concrete benefit immediately. Will it solve your weight problem entirely? Maybe not, but it will reform a negative behavior and have a positive result. Weaning yourself from eating late in the evening will eliminate high-calorie couch-potato snacking, give your digestion a chance to complete processing a day's worth of food (eight to ten hours), probably get you to bed earlier (because we eat to stay awake), improve the quality of your sleep (because it's more difficult to sleep on a full stomach), optimally balance the key hormones that support weight control (as these hormones require sleep longer than six hours to reach ideal levels), and ensure that you wake up with a good appetite for the day's most important meal (setting yourself up for steady energy until noon). The benefits from such a microresolution begin immediately and are yours forever.

Getting paid up front for your effort should leave you eager to nail your next resolution and its reward, so different from the familiar cycle of constantly renewing an ambitious and failed resolution in the hopes that you can finally achieve an ideal outcome *this time*. If your resolution delivers only after months of effort and you quit before you succeed, you end up empty-handed. For example, if you resolve *to be neat*, any day you're not completely neat means you've failed, and your frustration will lead you to give up before forming a single habit with a sustainable benefit. So when you next resolve *to be neat*, you have to start over at the very beginning. These resolution mulligans keep us from ever getting to other areas of self-improvement, because we haven't yet made any sustainable progress with our top priority.

Because each microresolution has an obvious intrinsic value, it's possible to comparison shop the benefits of potential resolutions and unambiguously design your progress in a given category of self-improvement. You might decide to follow up your resolution to make your bed each morning with a microresolution to hang up your work clothes every evening when you return from work, and you might then decide that the least neat thing you now do is to leave dishes in the sink long past mealtime and zero in on that. Part of the fun and dead-on utility of microresolutions is the ablity to forge a personal growth path.

You may decide to stick with *neat* until you've mastered every surface, ordered every closet, and organized your photo collections, or you may decide that you're happy enough with where *neat* is but that you'd really like to work on your fitness—what you tackle next depends on how your priorities evolve, given what you've been able to accomplish and what you believe will best enhance your life at a given moment. Microresolutions allow you to make progress in the sequence that benefits your life most, in contrast to resolutions that keep you treadmilling after an abstract goal such as *to be neat*, *to be organized*, or *to be financially responsible*.

A microresolution brings an immediate and valuable benefit, by design. Never think of your microresolution as an increment, merely a stepping-stone on the way to a future goal; the benefit your microresolution delivers today *is* the goal. Rejoice in the rewards that your microresolution provides today, and the future will take care of itself. Once you permanently lock in the benefits of just one behavioral change, you're on the path to continuous self-improvement.

CHAPTER 5

Made to Measure

S elf-improvement resolutions are amazingly consistent across generations and demographics; they are, it seems, timeless. No matter what our region, age, or ethnicity, the most important promise we make ourselves each year is selected from the same rack of tatty ready-to-wear resolutions that our grandparents browsed through two generations ago. These goals are so general that they suit broad swaths of the population—one-size-fits-all pledges. In contrast, a microresolution is made to measure for your individual circumstances, psyche, and history. A microresolution is bespoke, not mass market.

Rule 4: A Microresolution Is Personal

This book is full of examples to get you thinking, but to be effective, a microresolution must be designed by you, for you, based on observation of your own habits, attitudes, and situation. What personal behavior might you adopt, change, or eliminate to advance your objective? Thoughtfully analyze your habits to determine the single change that will have the biggest impact in your particular circumstances.

For example, at the New Year many will resolve *to be on time for work*, but solving late arrival will vary by individual. To design a resolution that gets *you* to work on time, examine the entire series of actions you take before you leave the house. Missing a train or bus by a second can mean a delay of fifteen minutes; driving into traffic five minutes behind schedule can mean arriving thirty minutes late (as anyone who commutes into Atlanta on I-285 can tell you). Oh, a minute is a lifetime in the morning! Every action counts, and time is wasted looking for keys, hunting for lunchbox items, finding a shoe, locating papers, counting out fare money, and dawdling over dressing decisions. Is your transit pass paid up? Do you need to get gas? Do you sometimes need to stop at the ATM on the way to work? If you are responsible for others in the morning, the opportunities to lose time multiply. Are you only just realizing that today is picture day at your kid's school? Wasn't there at least one more can of cat food yesterday?

Every routine morning action represents a unique opportunity to shave off minutes and gain an on-time advantage. A small change in habit can make all the difference. To improve my on-time record *without having to get up earlier*, I designed a series of microresolutions based on the actions I took each morning while preparing myself and my daughter for our daily commute in Manhattan, where I drop her at school and then go on to work.

My first "on time" microresolution focused on my activities just before leaving the house, which were often fraught. A successful morning exit means keys, cab cash, and a funded transit card in hand. Sometimes my keys were in a coat pocket, sometimes in a zipper pocket in my handbag, sometimes at the bottom of my bag, or sometimes upstairs on my bureau. Likewise, my transit card could be in a pocket or stuck in with my credit cards. My cash had often bafflingly dwindled below cab-fare levels, and at the last minute I would wind up scrabbling for coins in kitchen drawers and going through coat pockets in the hall closet. The exact amount remaining on my transit card was sometimes in doubt, and a refill required additional cash and a nerve-racking session with the ticket kiosk (New York's MTA ticket machines take credit cards, but the reader works only about 20 percent of the time). I can't tell you how many times I fumbled the funding of my transit card as the last "on time" train thundered by under our feet. So I resolved:

To prepare morning cash, keys, and transit card upon returning home from work

As I exited the train station each evening, I made sure that my transit card was funded for the morning. If I was short of cash, I stopped at an ATM on my way home. As soon as I stepped into the house, I put the cash, transit card, and keys together in a drawer near the front door. This action shaved minutes off our exit time, and I was less stressed during the entire morning routine because I stopped anticipating mishaps at the gate.

My new system worked, but keeping on top of cash and transit funding was high maintenance. I didn't have to refill my card or stop at the ATM every single day, but I had to think about whether or not I had to do these things, and that kept my new behavior from becoming truly autopilot. So I *tuned* my resolution to one I wouldn't have to think about more than once a week.

I began using a small change purse for cash and a transit card dedicated solely to the morning commute (and I tossed in a spare house key, just in case). I topped up the morning purse each Friday night for the following week and never used the cash or card in it for anything but the morning commute. I kept a different transit card for my midday, evening, and weekend trips in my wallet with the rest of my cash. When my wallet was empty I went to the cash machine, even if there was still cash in the morning purse. If I was out of fares on my "all purpose" transit card, I refilled it rather than "borrowing" from the morning card.

My daughter and I were never late again due to underfunded travel or MIA keys. For someone else (perhaps a guy with a wallet), the whole morning purse idea might seem silly, but for me it did the trick. Your microresolution for helping you get to work on time will be different from mine, because it will be personal to your habits and circumstances. Your opportunity to save time might be related to driving, carpooling, dressing, lunch making, child-care handoffs, or dog walking; it's by examining the personal sequence of your morning activities that you'll identify your first target. Or perhaps the greater on-time commuting pressure in your life is not on the way to work but on the way home, when last-minute work tasks, socializing, or errands put you behind to relieve your babysitter, get to class, or start dinner. If so, you'll be able to discover your first microresolution in the activities leading up to your departure and the actions you take en route.

Despite the hordes that swarm the latest crash diet, nothing is more personal than eating behaviors. The individual circumstances of why, how, where, when, what, and with whom we eat determine how many calories we end up consuming during the day. One person may eat late into the night; another skips breakfast; another eats his entire lunch while waiting in line to pay; another grazes continuously in party and bar scenes. It's these mindless eating behaviors that rob us of satisfaction and drive us to overeat. Finding the most effective resolution to begin reforming eating habits requires careful self-examination.

I was aware for many years that I ate quickly, certainly much faster than my slender husband, not to mention most of my other dining partners. Finished first, I felt cheated and unsatisfied while others continued to enjoy their meal, and I toyed with my empty plate, helped myself to seconds, or plowed through the bread basket. Even though I knew that the brain needs twenty minutes to register fullness, I generally finished eating in ten minutes or less. I wondered if I could break my habit of eating too fast by focusing a microresolution on it. I resolved:

To chew my food slowly

I found complying with my resolution exquisitely difficult. I had to remind myself constantly to slow down, and as soon as my concentration wandered, I sped up. Because I was narrowly focused on eating slowly, I was able to see for the first time how the rest of my dining habits posed obstacles to my success. From the vantage point of my resolution, I suddenly realized that all my dining actions were rushed—cutting my food, raising my fork to my mouth, drinking, using my napkin. I was trying to chew slowly, but in every other aspect I was racing. And—talk about personal—a bizarre and anxious thought kept occurring to me every time I tried to slow my eating: *If I don't speed up, I'll never be able to finish all this food.*

Clearly, at some point in my life, I had adopted the attitude that it was important to finish all, finish fast, and maybe even finish first. Perhaps my *chow-it-down* approach was the upshot of all those mornings I rushed away from the breakfast table to catch the school bus or fidgeted through our late family dinners, desperate to get away before prime time was over. Whatever the source of this attitude, it drove my eating behavior and clashed with my attempts to eat less because unconsciously I had placed a premium on the brisk completion of my task. Realizing that I was driven by the value of *speed* gave me the idea that the resolution would be more powerful if I *reframed* it to emphasize the value of slowness. My reframed resolution was:

To dine leisurely and savor my food and drink

Instead of telling myself to slow down, I told myself to savor and enjoy. I took each bite as if expecting a taste sensation, even if all I was eating was a banana. I savored the aroma, texture, and flavor of each bite and found that the flavor of the food intensified the longer I took to consume it. I would nibble at a small piece of chocolate and make it last, prolonging my enjoyment and increasing my satisfaction.

Cultivating the luxurious sensations of eating relaxed me, and I began to enjoy the feeling of leisure while dining, especially at dinner. I was reminded how satisfying it is to eat in France, where the portions are small, the food and atmosphere delightful, and the waitstaff never, ever rushes a diner. I thought about how saying grace shows appreciation for food and how that ritual of gratitude anticipates the pleasure and privilege of eating. I slowed down all my dining actions and stretched my time at the table, rather than bolting to clear up as soon as I had nothing left on my plate. I paid more attention to the nonfood elements of dinnertime—place settings, candles, and the like—so that the atmosphere was as pleasurable as the food. The longer dinner hour enhanced our time together as a family, rather than just filling up a slot in a day already jammed with activities.

My enjoyment so increased that I often found myself feeling

fully satisfied before I had finished my portion. *I consumed less, enjoyed more.* Consuming less and enjoying more became the benchmark for the dieting microresolutions I subsequently made. Each new resolution was guided by the experience of the last and was absolutely personal to my circumstances and psychology. I ended up losing fifteen pounds in about six months. And the key to my success was personal observation from start to finish.

The behaviors by which you save money are personal. Cameron and Gail loved to eat out often but recognized that it was becoming a budget breaker. They didn't want to give up eating out, so they made a resolution that when dining out on their own, they would skip bottled water and coffee, split a starter and a dessert, but each have their own main dish, resulting in a savings of about 30 percent per dining excursion. Their microresolution made it possible for them to continue to eat out regularly while spending less money (and consuming fewer calories).

How you relate to yourself is personal. In the midst of a painful divorce, Sarah found herself suddenly responsible for tasks her husband had managed before: taxes, bill paying, trip planning, finding and furnishing an apartment. For over twenty years her husband had taken responsibility for these basic survival activities. As her marriage had broken up when they were living abroad, she had no settled routine to return home to and had to build an entirely new life, including finding a job and a place to live.

On top of all the new practical realities that needed managing, Sarah also struggled with low spirits and self-esteem following the breakup. She knew she needed to galvanize herself to push through this painful period, but instead of bolstering herself with can-do messages, she was plagued by a negative, recurring thought. As soon as she would approach a task required to move her new life forward, she would find herself thinking, *I don't know what to do, I don't know what to do*, even if the next step was obvious. This negative message made her feel paralyzed and exhausted when she most needed to feel empowered and energized. Sarah searched for a microresolution message that could improve her mindset and create more positive energy around her endeavor. She resolved to send herself the message *I'm not helpless and I do know what to do*, whenever she felt overwhelmed by alien tasks or when negative thoughts about her ability to cope took possession of her mind. Whenever the *I don't know what to do* thought would occur to her, she would firmly repeat to herself, *I am not helpless and I do know what to do*. Now completely resettled, Sarah reports that her microresolution message has become a kind of mantra for this new period of freedom and responsibility. "Of course, I would have figured out how to get everything done even if I hadn't been sending myself this message, because I had to," she says. "But my microresolution message was important because it kept me from feeling like a victim, unworthy and incompetent, messages I realized I had been sending myself regularly but unwillingly. The message helped keep me on task and stopped me from brooding, and I got through what I had to do more quickly."

A microresolution is personal; it should fit like a glove. Or think of microresolution as a kind of remedy, a prescription you write for yourself. You're the doctor—start by examining your patient.

CHAPTER 6

Give It Some Spin

Once you've got a handle on the easy, limited, measurable, personal action of your microresolution, the next step is to *frame* your resolution statement. Framing is a semantic exercise, finding the language to concisely and accurately capture the action of your resolution and its cue. There's no exact formula for framing a resolution, but the most potent framings add perspective—a slant—to what you're trying to achieve. The framing should engage your mindset—your values, preferences, and outlook. The point isn't to be arty or clever but to strike the right psychological note by invoking meaningful values. Two people making essentially the same resolution will frame it differently, according to their unique perspectives and psychologies.

Rule 5: A Microresolution Resonates

If your resolution is a straightforward action cued by the clock or calendar, the most direct framing is the best—there's probably not much point in tinkering with *I resolve to walk to work on Monday mornings*. But resolutions with frequent and fluid cues can often be made more effective through a thoughtful and resonant framing. Consider a resolution discussed earlier in the book:

I resolve to chew my food slowly.　　　　　[Yuck.]

Reframed as:

I resolve to dine leisurely and savor my food and drink.　　　　　[Yum.]

Which of these two resolutions would you rather sign up for? The reframed resolution permanently transformed my eating mindset by focusing my dieting strategy on behaviors that foster enjoyment and celebration of mealtime. The new frame replaced a tacit admonishment (*Don't eat so fast*) with an affirmation (*Dining is a pleasure*). Instead of dutifully chewing my food to a slower metronomic setting, I came to the table anticipating the pleasure of giving every morsel luxurious attention. My resolution *to savor* taught me that it was critical to register and enjoy the act of eating, especially when trying to eat less. Thanks to this reframing I realized that

mindful eating = greater satisfaction = less food consumption

Understanding the connection between mindfulness and satisfaction led me to make a series of *mindful-eating* resolutions (see chapter 12, "Diet and Nutrition") that fundamentally altered my eating behaviors and led to permanent weight loss. On its own, a spot-on framing can produce smart and actionable insights.

This rest of this chapter is devoted to discussing how framing strategies can be used to create more effective microresolutions. You'll discover that a canny framing can make a tremendous difference in your outlook and motivation—that it can literally change your frame of mind.

The Power of Positive Framing

Most of us would rather follow a positive directive than a negative one. A resolution *not to snack* is pretty dismal; the microresolution message *I enjoy dinner so much more when I'm hungry for it* steers the tempted snacker toward a more gratifying goal. The reframing expresses a positive value (I enjoy sitting down to an evening meal with good appetite) rather than simply stressing a negative one (snacking is bad). The resolution's open framing encourages taking any and all actions that foster good appetite at mealtime: Limiting snacks, choosing lighter snacks, timing snacks better, eating a moderate lunch, and increasing exercise all fit within the message frame. Since this is a message aimed at mindset, success is measured simply by remembering to give yourself the message when you're tempted to overeat in the hours before dinner, and if you arrive at mealtime hungry, you know the message has done its work.

Let's examine how you might frame a resolution that targets your working life. For nearly any professional, learning how to receive and use feedback is critical to advancement, and defensiveness in the face of negative feedback is seen as a sign of immaturity. Your first instinct might be to resolve *not to be defensive when receiving feedback from the boss*, but that's simply a prohibition; it doesn't encourage a more constructive response. A better framing might be *to listen, acknowledge, and give thoughtful consideration to feedback from the boss.* This restatement promotes the positive values of listening, acknowledging, and thoughtfulness. If the positive value of *thoughtful consideration* doesn't completely quash your impulse to justify yourself, you can add to your resolution that you will wait twenty-four hours before responding. The waiting period will stymie your compulsion to play *block that feedback* while leaving the door open to engage your boss later with a considered response. The waiting period will also give you time to reflect on whether it's worth going on record with an objection (most often it isn't). The frame could also be broadened to *I will listen, acknowledge, and give thoughtful consideration to feedback at work*, that is, feedback coming from all quarters: the boss, colleagues, clients, and subordinates. But if you struggle with defensiveness in general and know you will find this difficult, keep the frame narrow: Start with the boss and then expand your resolution once you get the hang of listening instead of arguing (and explaining is arguing). And cheer yourself with the thought that you're not alone:

> The trouble with most of us is that we would rather be
> ruined by praise than saved by criticism.
>
> —Norman Vincent Peale, *The Power of Positive Thinking*
> (Simon & Schuster, 1952)

Let's turn to a different example from family life. Many parents would like to increase the time they devote to meaningful activities with their children. If Sunday is generally your family day but often just dissipates into late breakfasts, puttering, and individual activities, you might want to design a microresolution that will make Sundays count. Your initial framing might be simply *to spend time with the kids every Sunday afternoon;* yet this resolution might be more attractively reframed as *to plan a fun Sunday outing with the kids on Friday night.* The reframed resolution is better in several respects—the first framing seems to be all about obligation and compartmentalization, while the second framing emphasizes going out and having a good time, and the Friday planning session with the kids could prove to be a fun event all on its own. The Friday night confab also guarantees that a specific plan will be set in motion before weekend inertia sets in first thing on Saturday morning.

Casting your resolution in a positive light increases motivation by helping to dispel the negative attitudes that impede progress. Seeing the glass as half full rather than half empty is a great approach to life and a powerful habit worth cultivating on its own. Framing your resolutions in affirmative language promotes that upbeat spin.

The Power of Zero-Tolerance Framing

Positivity is nearly always the best strategy for framing, but not always. If your resolution focuses on a small action (taken or un-taken) that can lead to or prevent a slide into disorder, consider using the language of *zero tolerance* to frame it. Each one of us can probably point to seemingly trivial actions of our own that get us into disproportionate trouble. Some people may be able to eat just a few potato chips at a party and then walk away, but for those for whom the salty, rich taste of one chip leads to eating handfuls, a resolution to have *zero tolerance for eating chips at parties* might be in order. For many the "quick" check of e-mail at 11:00 p.m. can mean not hitting the sack until 1:00 a.m.—once mesmerized by the screen, they free-associate their way around the Internet, Googling facts from the TV program they just watched, logging into Facebook to see if an ex-girlfriend's status has changed, starting a chat with a friend spotted online. The computer revives and stimulates them, the opportunity for a good night's sleep slips away, and when the alarm rings they awaken to misery and remorse. A resolution to have *zero tolerance for leisure computing after 10:00 p.m.* acknowledges the danger of even a quick pre-bedtime visit to cyberspace. The "leisure" caveat in the framing recognizes that legitimate work will sometimes require a late-night computer session.

The first time I used the language of zero tolerance in framing a resolution was after I moved from my Manhattan apartment to a Brooklyn brownstone. The sink in the master bathroom was set into a very large marble countertop. I took one look at all that surface and immediately resolved to have *zero tolerance for any items left out on the counter.* In my previous apartment I'd had just a freestanding sink, so my laziness in returning items to the medicine chest had been checked by the limited surface. Now, face to face with my vast new bathroom counter, I knew that if I didn't make a *zero-tolerance* resolution to keep its surface clear, soon my moisturizer, hand lotion, sunblock, makeup, toothbrush, toothpaste, dental floss, blow-dryer, and hair-grooming aids would take up permanent residence there. For months I zealously practiced my resolution, tolerating not a single Q-tip, aspirin bottle, or bobby pin on the sink console. Every time I walked into my bathroom and saw that big empty surface, I felt gratified.

The adage "a stitch in time saves nine" is cousin to zero-tolerance logic. For people who absolutely depend on their cell phones, going to bed without recharging can be disastrous. The small inaction of not plugging in the phone overnight can blow up the next day—professionally, when clients, colleagues, and superiors can't get in touch, and personally, when a partner, sitter, child, doctor, or teacher has an urgent need to make contact.

Resolving to have *zero tolerance for going to bed without charging the cell phone* means that if you've already gone to bed, turned out the light, and started to fall asleep before you realize you haven't plugged in the phone, you force yourself to get up and do it. (A friend of mine who often neglected to charge his phone solved his problem by tossing his alarm clock and opting instead to depend on his phone to wake him in the morning. His solution to the uncharged phone was to double down on phone dependence. He still had to build the habit of making sure his phone was charged, but he upped the stakes and picked up a new phone-charging cue—setting the alarm before bed.)

When Peter, who had always lived out of his car—the backseat filled with books, newspapers, half-consumed drinks, kid items, and gym clothes—purchased a new car, he resolved to have *zero tolerance for leaving anything in the car at the end of the day*. This framing led him not only to clear the car of books, files, papers, and the like each evening but also to hunt down tiny violations like gum wrappers and stray Cheerios that had escaped his child's grasp in the backseat. Using the zero-tolerance framing was much more effective for him than simply resolving *to keep the car clean*. A car—someone else's car—with a few things items in it can still be neat, but the proud owner of this new car knew that leaving behind a single item would begin his steep descent into total sloth.

Use zero-tolerance framing only for situations where such vigilance—even zealotry—is necessary to guard against the misstep that leads to indulgence, lack of control, true disorder. If you know that eating one peanut in the bar means eating the whole bowl, or that clicking on the sample-sale pop-up ad will lead to a cart full of purchases you can't afford, or that a dead lightbulb will be left unchanged until many more burnouts leave you in the gloom, consider a zero-tolerance approach. But use this framing sparingly, so that it retains its punch. Zero tolerance is best for resolutions involving actions that can be accomplished very quickly, probably within five minutes. Keep it for the stitch that saves nine.

The Power of Suggestion

The rich imagination and innate empathy of human beings leave them vulnerable to suggestion. A memorable or resonant phrase heard over and over can penetrate one's consciousness and alter attitudes, even values. Just ask the Mad Men who spend their days trying to get into your head with a clever slogan, catchy jingle, or modish logo. Political campaigns use suggestion to undermine public confidence in a candidate's suitability for office. The hypnotist artfully plants new attitudes in the mind of a patient who is trying to quit smoking. Police use suggestion in interrogation to steer a suspect toward confession—sometimes so successfully that an innocent person confesses to a crime he didn't commit.

Children are even more suggestible than adults, which is why childhood is a great training ground for building habits and mindset. We've all heard the expression *children are sponges*, meaning that kids soak up whatever is in their environment without a filter. Because children are so easily influenced by suggestion, the values and attitudes taught by parents have deep and lasting effects, both positive and negative. Each of us can probably quote dozens of aphorisms impressed on us in childhood that are an active part of our mindset today: *If you want something, you must work for it. You'll get more attention if you sit in the front row. The early bird gets the worm. Nobody likes a sore loser. Honesty is the best policy. Don't be a crybaby. Clean your plate; other children are starving.* Our moral education teaches us not only through example and exhortation but also through repetition of memorable maxims such as the Golden Rule.

The aphorisms learned in childhood shape more than the character of individuals; they shape the character of entire nations. *Keep a stiff upper lip*—the British version of *Don't be a crybaby*—is core to British identity, associated not just with national stoicism but also with British physiognomy. Kristen Linklater, the celebrated voice teacher from the UK who trained a generation of Shakespearean actors and authored the classic *Freeing the Natural Voice*, writes about the hard work of unfreezing stiff upper lips in adult actors who learned to mask their emotions by translating this common maxim into physical reality. (One might wonder what effect another famous British expression, "Keep buggering on,"—referred to by Churchill simply as *KBO*—had on the British population!)

Suggestion is a powerful force we can exploit for ourselves, not just use to influence others. A *microresolution message* is a suggestion you design to get inside your own head and change your mindset. The purpose of the message is to work directly on your values, preferences, and attitudes. Since the power of a microresolution message lies entirely in its suggestive power, its framing is critical. If the message hits its mark and resonates, over time the message will change your mindset and transform your actions.

As with a slogan, a jingle, or a childhood lesson, the idea is to come up with a catchy dispatch that resonates through the artful use of suggestion. Like the most memorable aphorisms of childhood, a snappy message is the most effective. Brevity and acuity help the suggestion—your note to self—get deep into your head and pop up in response to the circumstance you select as your cue.

So let's examine how you might influence yourself through

the art of suggestion. As discussed in an earlier chapter, the first microresolution message I tried on myself was to say, *It's really just as fast to hang it up,* when I was taking off my coat in the evening. Seems a straightforward and obvious phrasing, right? But I might have framed the message in several different ways:

1. Oh, just hang it up, for Christ's sake!
2. Don't be such a slob; hang it up!
3. You'll only have to hang it up later, so why not just do it now?
4. Dropping it in the chair and then hanging it up later takes longer than just hanging it up in the first place.
5. It's just as fast to hang it up.
6. It's really just as fast to hang it up.

Framings 1 and 2 are similar—exhortations to a lazy slob to get with the program. Framings 3 through 6 are similar in logic (you don't really save time by dropping a coat on a chair) but different in tone and length. Framings 5 and 6 are almost identical, but the insertion of the word "really" in 6 shades the statement to mean that, all in all, it's virtually as fast to hang it up, and "really" also captures a little of the exasperation expressed in framings 1 and 2.

At the time I took up this microresolution message, I had not only the habit of dropping my coat on a living room chair when I came home but also the habit of dropping my clothes on a bedroom chair when I undressed for bed. The suggestion that *it's really just as fast to hang it up* resulted, over time, in a change in mindset that had multiple results. First, I grew to believe, *through experience*, that it is really just as fast to hang it up. Then the suggestion chipped away at my *speedy* = *efficient* mindset by demonstrating that some "shortcuts" actually cost more time, because they require remedial action later; and while the cue I used to trigger the message was the removal of my coat, over time the message's suggestive power spread, cropping up in my head every time I removed an article of clothing, until the bedroom chair was stripped down to its birthday suit and I could actually sit in it. The *just as fast* suggestion now pops up all the time in other contexts, as in: *It's really just as fast to file it.*

As discussed in the introduction, each new habit is a model that the mind can reuse and build upon. Once you experience that hanging up your coat immediately is actually faster than dropping it in a chair and returning to hang it up later, it's not a big leap to see that it's faster to file a receipt immediately than to toss it in a pile and deal with it a month on. One successful new habit can break the hold that general inertia may have on a given area of self-improvement, leading us to learn faster, operate more intelligently, and progress more swiftly.

Now let's take a look at a workplace example concerning a person who has received feedback that his dismissive attitude toward his colleagues is contributing to low morale. Consider which of the following message framings would be most effective in curtailing this toxic habit:

1. Put-downs aren't nice.
2. Put-downs are a sign of insecurity.
3. Put-down artists are pathetic.
4. Put-downs are unprofessional.
5. There's no such thing as a professional put-down.

All of these framings *suggest* a perspective on the negative value of put-downs. The first framing is pretty bland; of course, a person who compulsively puts others down knows it isn't *nice*, so this message isn't likely to resonate in a way that brings a change in mindset. Numbers 2 and 3, by suggesting that put-downs are a symptom of weakness, undermine the swagger and sense of superiority that come with dismissing others, and 4 and 5 cast the action of put-downs as unprofessional. Individuals will react differently to the framing choices above, and each must shoot the arrow most likely to strike his or her psychological bull's-eye. But for me, 5 has the most punch; the notion of professionalism resonates with me, and this framing's fine-tuned semantics make it plain that there is no put-down that qualifies as a professional response to a colleague's idea. Disagreements are professional; insults are not. Again, what works for one person won't work for another. Look for the suggestion that really pushes your button.

Size Matters

If your microresolution initiates an activity that you can choose to schedule more or less frequently, consider whether it is more advantageous to batch up the activity or break it into smaller increments. For example, if you hate doing laundry and let it pile up until it becomes a mountain, you might find that it's actually less onerous to follow through if you resolve to do small loads on a more frequent schedule rather than leaving it all for a marathon session once a month. Similarly, you might need to pay bills only once in a monthly cycle, but you might prefer to set aside one night each week for administrative tasks so that your home in-box stays empty and your mind stress free. Conversely, something you do very frequently might better be managed in a batch, freeing up time slots to accomplish other goals.

Playing with the frequency of an activity often leads to surprising results.

Nancy's goal was to call her widowed father three times a week, but she often ended up calling only once. The first five minutes of the call were usually devoted to hearing out her father's rants about how difficult life was becoming. She began to dread these calls; she usually hung up feeling guilty and wiped out from absorbing so much anger. She began finding more and more excuses to put the calls off, leaving larger gaps in her calling schedule than she could feel good about. So Nancy made a microresolution to call her father every day but to keep the call short, even if that meant ending the call while her dad was still in the rant zone. To her surprise, the tenor of the calls improved tremendously. Because very little time had passed between calls, her father's list of frustrations was shorter, and overall his mood and tone were markedly more upbeat. Because she was calling more frequently, she didn't have to struggle to reserve a half hour for the call; she just called whenever she had five or ten minutes free. Nancy realized after several weeks that the complaints that used to mark the beginning of every chat had been a placeholder for her father's core frustration—he wanted his children to check in with him more often. She began enjoying her talks with her father, because the daily calls made him so much cheerier.

My friend Ethan made a microresolution to do one push-up a day. At first his resolution worked well, as *assuming the position* was most of the battle. Once he began, he often went well beyond his just-one commitment. Soon he found himself doing twenty push-ups a day. Successful microresolution? No, because Ethan stopped. Why? Because even though he had resolved to do only one daily push-up, as that number grew, so did his expectations; he soon felt he must do twenty every day, a resolution he had never signed up for. The one push-up a day was a great stratagem for getting back in the swing of doing push-ups, and doing just one at first produced value because he was so out of practice. But once he gained in strength and endurance, the one-push-up resolution simply became a proxy for a more ambitious yet undefined resolution. From that point on, Ethan was practicing a resolution without limits, breaking rule 1.

Don't let the can-do spirit fostered by your *easy* microresolution lead to scope creep. If you've practiced your resolution for a while and you want to do more, think it through and recommit; don't make it up as you go along. Keep yourself out of the ad hoc decision space; make explicit commitments you know you can keep.

Ethan might have reframed his push-up resolution with respect to the number of repetitions as soon as he realized that a single push-up was no longer a real goal delivering real value. He might have reformulated his resolution as twenty push-ups two days a week. That would have been a huge advance over the zero push-ups he had been doing pre–microresolution and would have left the door open for doing additional sets on other days as the spirit moved him. Remember, making a microresolution to do push-ups on Tuesdays and Saturdays before breakfast doesn't mean that you can't do push-ups more often; it means only that you have an ironclad commitment to do twenty push-ups according to your resolution schedule and that you measure your success only against that standard. While it makes sense to reconsider a batching strategy as you gain in efficiency and experience once you're past the *test-drive* period (see chapter 9, "Test-Driving Your Resolution"), you should stick with a resolution for at least four weeks before revisiting the size of your commitment. And if you do decide to up your batch, don't get carried away by irrational exuberance—remember rule 1 and keep your microresolution easy.

A deft framing can make a big difference in the impact of your resolution, and you'll be surprised how much you learn about yourself in the process of selecting a frame. A microresolution's cue is also part of its framing but is so important a topic that rule 6 is devoted entirely to it.

CHAPTER 7

Trigger Happy

We awake to the sound of the alarm; we perk up at the smell of morning coffee; we rush through the turnstile when we feel the rumble of the train approaching; we grab leftover pizza from an open box on an office desk; we click on a pop-up ad for a snazzy phone; we call out, "I'm home," when we pass through the front door; we head up to bed when the late news beams at us from the TV screen. We spend our lives reacting to *cues*, automatically responding with a learned behavior pattern in a specific situation or context.

Rule 6: A Microresolution Fires on Cue

Cues are personal—two people who each snack at the same time every afternoon may be responding to entirely different cues. The cue for one person may be a hunger pang; for another, it's passing the vending machine on the way out of the gym locker room. The first time you make a purchase from the vending machine, you may feel real hunger, but if you repeat the pattern of gym plus vending-machine purchase enough times, soon the mere sight of the machine will prompt you to make a purchase.

Behavioral research demonstrates that it is the strong association between behavior and cue that creates a lasting habit.*

Linking the action of your microresolution to a cue is critical to making your new behavior automatic. Cues are discovered, not invented—the cue for your resolution already exists, you just need to identify it. It may be internal (hunger, drowsiness, an impulse to scold), or environmental (the smell of freshly fried doughnuts, a shoe display in a shop window, criticism received from a coworker).

Advertisers have long been expert at identifying cues that entice particular demographics; now they can analyze your Internet behavior and serve up a cue designed exclusively for *you*. Advertisers profile not only your Internet content preferences but also the visuals and advertising approaches most likely to trigger your coveted click. It's galling to get ads for reducing belly fat (all those diet articles you click on, the clothing sizes you order) or to have an ad flash in your face for a pair of shoes you recently deleted from your shopping cart in a hard-won act of self-discipline. Now that pair of shoes follows you wherever you go on the Web, sometimes even walking right toward you in an animation designed to capture your attention and your click. Yep, online advertisers have your number when it comes to the cues you respond to, and they can serve up content in a way that makes your mouse finger itch. The more you click, the smarter advertisers become about which cues are likely to catch your eye. (I try to resist clicking on trashy Internet news stories—LINDSAY LOHAN BACK IN JAIL! HALF-TON WOMAN CHARGED WITH MURDER!—because I can't bear to think about the silly profile I am building up in cyberspace and the

---

* Kathleen D. Vohs et al., "Making Choices Impairs Subsequent Self-Control: A Limited-Resource Account of Decision Making, Self-Regulation, and Active Initiative," *Journal of Personality and Social Psychology* 94, no. 5 (May 2008): 883–98.

onslaught of human-degradation stories building in the pipeline especially for me.)

An essential part of framing your resolution is identifying the cue best suited to trigger the action you've committed to perform. If your resolution is tied to the clock or calendar, the cue will be fairly obvious. Returning to our old favorite, *Walk to work on Monday mornings*, if you're walking from home to work, the cue is *leaving the house on Monday morning*; if you've resolved to walk from a certain bus stop, the cue to begin walking is when the bus pulls up at the designated stop. If you make the fitness resolution *to climb six flights of stairs every workday after lunch*, then getting up from the lunch table is your cue to head for the stairwell. Notice that in these two examples, the action isn't cued simply by the hands of the clock but by actions already associated with the time of day. This gives the cue greater definition and dimension, making it easier to pick up. For example, the resolution to *plug in my cell phone before bed* would work better as *plug in my cell phone before brushing my teeth at night*—because the second you pick up your toothbrush (cue) you can check yourself, rather than leaving your recharge action to shuffle around in the elastic time zone known as *before bed*.

If your new behavior can't be tied to a day or time but is triggered by context, discovering the ideal cue might prove challenging. Sometimes the easiest way to cue a new behavior is to piggyback it on an established habit. The existing habit acts as a "string around the finger," reminding you of your resolution until it in turn becomes automatic. As discussed earlier in this book, I used piggybacking to link a new behavior to my habit of checking e-mail; since then I've used the same strategy many times to establish a sturdy cue for a new habit.

When I first started practicing my notebook habit, the cue to take out my notebook was *the impulse to make a note*, which might occur at any moment in the meeting. Pausing to dig out my notebook created an annoying break in meeting flow, so I began using the action of slipping off my handbag as the cue, that is, I *piggybacked* the notebook action on the handbag one. Had I ever before thought of the act of removing my handbag as a habit? Not at all; I never thought about it at all because it was part of autopilot. But once you start scrutinizing your established routines for potential cues, you'll begin to realize just how programmed most of your actions are. Any bit of that programming can be used as an anchor for a new behavior you're trying to establish. If you want to acquire the habit of drinking eight glasses of water a day, you might decide that each time you wash your hands, you're going to drink a glass of water. As most of us wash our hands eight times a day, drinking a glass of water after each washing should easily satisfy an eight-glass quota. The selected cue also makes performing the resolution easier, as water is at hand when the cue fires.

The cuing examples discussed above involve establishing a cue for a new behavior (organized note taking, water drinking), and thus the choice of cue is discretionary. But when you make a resolution with the goal of disrupting an established behavior such as snacking, defensiveness, or impulse buying, cue discovery becomes more complex. You may uncover multiple triggers for your habit, and you'll need to choose one to serve as the cue for your microresolution. Don't try to include all the possible cues in your framing or you'll fall into the *wannabe* trap of thinking you can change a load of ingrained behavioral responses overnight.

For example, if your goal is to limit your snacking, make a list of cues that trigger your desire to snack. If you see pizza left out after a meeting, does it cue you to take a slice? What about a box of chocolates on a colleague's desk? If you come into work satisfied from your breakfast and see free doughnuts, will you likely take one anyway? As soon as you begin to prepare a meal, do you begin to nosh? When you clear up from a meal, does left-over food on the plates of others trigger a round of snacking right after you've just eaten? What about your response to seeing bar and party food once you begin to drink? When you hit the su-permarket, do you immediately begin looking for free samples? Or is your cue to snack the feeling of absolute lethargy that comes over you at around 3:00 p.m.? Or do you experience hunger pangs around 4:30 p.m.? An organized list of such cues might look like this:

1. Unsought workplace treats (doughnuts, chocolates, pizzas)
2. Market samples
3. Food you prepare for others
4. Leftovers on the plates of others
5. Bar snacks
6. Party snacks
7. Afternoon hunger
8. Exhaustion

Considering cues 1 and 2, you might make a resolution not to indulge when you encounter snack pop-ups at the office or mar-ket (resolving to foreswear free food in these environments and instead always buy your own); cues 3 and 4 would help frame a resolution establishing boundaries between the food you serve yourself and the food served to others; cues 5 and 6 invite making a resolution to limit food grazing in the proximity of drinks. The physically generated cues 7 and 8 are entirely different from the first six environmentally generated cues. Cue 7 requires a strat-egy for staving off hunger between meals without overindulging (e.g., *I resolve to eat a piece of whole fruit at 3:00 p.m.*); cue 8, exhaustion, suggests a number of remedies, from more sleep at night to a catnap to consuming a limited chemical pick-me-up such as coffee and sugar (50 calories) rather than a more destructive treat such as a brownie (450 calories).

Once you observe the breadth of these snacking cues, you'll begin to see how large a resolution *to stop snacking* really is, because our environment is constantly churning out cues to eat. To make a resolution you are certain you can keep, focus your resolution on one specific cue (or logical cue pair) at a time. For example, you might first resolve not to eat any sugary, opportunistic treats at the office (preserving the optionality of the pizza slice) and several weeks later resolve not to eat off the plates of others. Each resolution will reduce the number of opportunities to snack until you've reached a level of control that works for you.

Sometimes it makes sense to abstract the framing of a resolution to cover cues that are very similar. I once made a resolution not to eat in line; later I amended it to not eat in transit; later it became a resolution to eat only when sitting down (with exceptions for ice cream cones and cocktail parties with canapés). The situations that led me into mindless eating—eating in line while waiting to pay for food, wolfing down lunch while rushing to a meeting, eating while cooking, grazing in party scenes— were so closely related that framing a single resolution to cover all of these cues made sense. Note, however, that I started with one cue (waiting in line) and then added cues over many weeks until I ended up with a resolution that covered all of the situations: *to eat only when seated.*

The very act of cue discovery often leads to insights worth acting on. For example, I once thought about a resolution to break myself of the habit of second helpings. I thought about what stimulated the desire to eat more even though I had already consumed a satisfying meal. I realized the cue for serving myself more was not hunger, not desire, but my empty plate. Taking a cue from *the cue*, I resolved *to always leave something on my plate*. The portion-control battle was refocused on just that last bite, not another plate of food or second scoop of ice cream. Even if you serve yourself a slightly larger portion so that you'll have something to leave behind, training yourself not *to clean your plate* (to say nothing of not licking the plate) will change your mindset by visually demonstrating that a meal is done when you're satisfied, not when your plate is empty. Seeing your plate removed with something tasty on it is a mental game changer and a strategy that applies to so many areas where one might wish more self-control: refusing another drink while you're still wide awake and sober, going to bed before you're staggering from exhaustion, ending your shopping spree while you still have plenty of discretionary cash in your budget, quitting an argument before it escalates.

Relationship cues are often volatile, subtle, and more difficult to recognize. The cue for a habitual reaction may be an unanticipated communication, a rush of strong feeling, or a sudden impulse, and that fleeting cue must be caught and processed quickly. What's the cue to guilt-trip your partner, rage at a child, undermine a colleague, or snap at an older parent? What's the cue for putting yourself down or one-upping a friend? Such cues can be slippery and require careful identification.

Let's return to the *defensiveness* example and think through how one might zero in on what cues this negative habit. Defensiveness shows as a specific reaction to a specific circumstance. Defensive with the boss is different from defensive with a colleague, friend, lover, child, parent. You have to solve for defensiveness one situational cue at a time. Trying to come up with one big *I will not be defensive* resolution to respond to an onslaught of varied cues will very likely fail. But as you practice responding less defensively in one situation, the next situation you tackle will prove less difficult, and your resolved response will take hold more quickly.

The model of pairing an identified cue with a resolved response works for any relationship dynamic that you want to disrupt. If you're a doormat who constantly pleases others at your own expense, learning how to break the habit of saying yes before considering any of the personal consequences begins by thinking through the situations that put you on the spot. Feeling railroaded into a movie you don't want to see is very different from feeling pressured to cover for a lax employee. If you've always followed a strategy of pleasing to succeed, it will take fortitude and practice to give yourself permission to displease others by saying no. Therefore, you must carefully consider the situational cues that put pressure on you to say yes, and select the one you think most important to nail first. It might be a cue that comes up between you and your love interest (to make dinner instead of eating out), a crushing parental demand (to spend your entire vacation at the old homestead), or a dump of work from a colleague on Friday night (the "almost finished" project you're handed that is light-years away from being done). You might choose to deal with the situation that's the easiest to handle (*"Let's go out to dinner so we can both relax"*) or select the target with the most life impact (*"I don't have time to help you finish your project tonight"*). Note the absence of the word "sorry" from this last example. "Sorry" is more than unnecessary; it's counterproductive. "Sorry" only reinforces your sense of obligation/guilt and communicates to the slacker that you are in the wrong for not helping. It's business, not personal, and with respect to this business task, you aren't in a position to help, period. Changing a habitual response isn't a snap; you'll have to practice and practice (drill, baby, drill) until you feel the merit of your new response, it begins to feel natural, and you realize you can survive the disappointment of others. It's at that point you're ready to tackle other situations that cue your doormat tendencies.

Once you get clued into cues, your heightened awareness will provide fresh insight into internal and external triggers, so that you learn to pick out the best cue for each resolution. Establishing a strong link between an action and its cue is essential for making a new behavior automatic, and a careful framing overall will help you nail your resolution and make practicing it more enjoyable. A microresolution can turn into a real adventure, leading you into unfamiliar psychological territory where personal discoveries are made.

CHAPTER 8

Practice Makes Permanent

E xperiencing the power of microresolutions may inspire you to double down on a mega set of micros. Resist that suicidal impulse. Less is more when it comes to achieving lasting change. It takes concentration to nurture a fresh attitude, adopt a new habit, or drop a negative behavior. Effectively changing one's formula for living is a rarity, a behavioral breakthrough.

Rule 7: Make Microresolutions
Just Two at a Time

Two celebrated behavioral researchers once famously summarized the foundation of their science thusly:

> Most of the time what we do is what we do most of the time. Sometimes we do something new.*

Doing something new, something differently, demands *rigor*.

---

* David J. Townsend and Thomas G. Bever, *Sentence Comprehension: The Integration of Habits and Rules* (A Bradford Book, 2001), 2.

Your microresolution is *easy* only in the sense that it is clearly achievable, but establishing any new behavior requires *rigor*. You must be in a position to demand of yourself that you follow through on your commitment, and that won't be possible if you overreach. Building a positive new behavior requires attention and self-control, both limited resources. If you try to change too much too fast, you'll be overwhelmed, lose your concentration, fumble cues, and end up with only patchy compliance. A habit isn't a habit until it's a habit—you have to go after it with single-minded purpose until you get it into autopilot. To guarantee unwavering focus and success, make your resolutions no more than two at a time.

Limiting your resolutions ensures that you have the attention and endurance to stick with a behavioral shift until it becomes autopilot. What creates a habit is repeating a behavior over time in association with a specific context. As habit researchers David Neal and Wendy Wood have observed, "[Habits] are acquired *gradually* as people *repeatedly respond* in a recurring context."*

A new habit needs time to work its way into autopilot and become neurologically embedded. Your microresolution will take around four weeks before it begins to feel less awkward and six to eight weeks before it begins to feel natural. Four to six weeks is what I've experienced as an average, but each microresolution is unique and challenging in a different way, so there's no absolute rule. A microresolution that you practice daily might start feeling sticky at three weeks, but another resolution practiced less frequently may still feel pretty raw at eight. You may start two resolutions at the same time, but they won't necessarily finish on the same schedule.

---

* D. T. Neal et al., "How Do Habits Guide Behavior? Perceived and Actual Triggers of Habits in Daily Life," *Journal of Experimental Social Psychology* 48, no. 2 (2011): 492–98 (emphasis added).

But as soon as one of your resolutions is solid and isn't taxing to maintain, you can start working on a new one. As you take up new microresolutions, your previous resolutions will continue to work themselves into true autopilot over a period of months.

Don't make the mistake of confusing your resolution to behave differently with actually having achieved a change in habit. A decision to do something isn't the same thing as doing it; habit is a product of practice, not definition. Just because you decide to make the bed each morning doesn't mean you now have the habit of making the bed. Pledging not to say "I told you so" isn't the same thing as actually stifling the impulse to say it (or its equivalent) whenever you are proved correct (by your lights). Habits and insight are products of experience; rushing through your resolution to check the "done" box only stunts your learning and deprives your new habit of a strong foundation. One reason microresolutions work is that success is so narrowly defined that failure just isn't an option. If all you are working on is one or two limited changes in behavior, you can force yourself to account. When you load yourself up, you let yourself off the hook.

Some microresolutions take longer than eight weeks. I consciously practiced *to dine leisurely and savor my food and drink* longer than any of my other resolutions, but I was well rewarded for the time invested. My slower eating pace became the behavioral cornerstone of all the other eating resolutions I made that led (at last) to my permanent weight loss. My habit of rushing was so deeply rooted that as soon as my concentration wandered, I would find myself speeding up. I realized during this period of trying to eat more slowly that I rushed in everything I did—walking, working, thinking, cooking, speaking. Indeed, I had made such a virtue of hurrying that I hurried even when I was on vacation and supposedly relaxing. Once I realized that my rushing was often more fetishistic than strategic, I consciously began to slow myself down in situations where speeding created no value or was actually counterproductive. I wouldn't have been able to retrain my eating habits or understand my rushing mindset if I had skipped ahead to my next resolution before mastering the habit of conscious eating.

During the four or five months it took the *savor my food* resolution to stick, I was able to make three other microresolutions in the "second slot," so progress continued on new fronts while I chipped away at speed eating. So even if a resolution takes more than eight weeks to master, you'll still be able to keep working on other resolutions at the same time. At this point I've made and kept so many microresolutions that it seems silly to worry about limiting myself to two—averaging about five weeks per resolution, two at time, that's twenty resolutions you can make this year that will utterly change your life. And the value of those resolutions will compound—as you begin to replace bad behaviors with good ones, positive new behaviors will emerge on their own, driven by a mindset revitalized by new experiences.

If focusing on two microresolutions at the same time proves a struggle, cut back to just one until you have a handle on what it takes to build a new behavior. Don't underestimate your achievement in creating just a single new habit. If you're working one or two resolutions at a time, you'll be doing something new all the time, so it's just daft to let yourself become impatient with the pace of change.

As a rule of thumb, keep resolutions that are practiced daily for at least four weeks and resolutions practiced less frequently for eight weeks before making new ones. Each resolution should feel like a behavior you don't ever want to do without before you make your next commitment. Don't rush. If you carefully establish your new habit, it will last a lifetime, so who cares about a few extra weeks? As you take up new resolutions, your old ones must continue working for you—no backsliding. Never add to commitments you're struggling with—you only risk short-circuiting your gains and undermining your confidence in your ability to follow through without excuses.

"*But*," you might well ask, "*what about those times when I feel completely inspired and just want to take a direct run at total transformation?*" Well, then, by all means, *go for it*, but keep faith with your microresolutions at the same time. Don't get confused about your dual efforts. A microresolution is about making a fundamental behavioral shift for a lifetime, not throwing a Hail Mary to try to win in the last three seconds of the final quarter.

There are times when the *wannabe* resolution can succeed, when the stars align and transformation is achieved through sweat and inspiration. Such inspiration is often fueled by a personal crisis—getting dumped motivates a weight loss; a health scare demands an end to smoking; a bad job review leads to a pristine desk; a financial debacle forces frugality on a spendthrift. The *midlife crisis* is often a time of change, when fear of decline leads to new regimens designed to recapture health and youthfulness. I was interested to see a famous and wonderfully talented actor, a total beefcake until he fattened significantly in his midthirties, suddenly slim down in his fifties. Told by his doctor that he was becoming diabetic, the panicked actor gave up all sugar immediately. He lost forty-five pounds in three months from a single change in behavior that he took on only because of a medical scare. Twenty years of a growing waistline and funky character roles, and then . . . *Shazaam!* Rehunked! While it's important to respond to life's turning points with energy and determination, why wait for fate to dish up a dire cue before you take action? Remember, the goal is sustainable self-improvement, not intermittent bursts of drastic action (aka New Year's resolutions).

Successful savers started early and started small. They began with pennies, graduated to dimes, and then continued to quarters. They didn't tell themselves that saving a sawbuck wouldn't amount to a million dollars. Rather, they made saving a habit, and over time that habit bred other financially sound behaviors and attitudes. Microresolutions work the same way. Continuously work one or two microresolutions at a time, and you'll enter a state of continuous self-improvement, reaching ambitious goals that you once thought unattainable.

CHAPTER 9

Test-Driving Your Resolution

It's time to take your new microresolution for a spin and see how it drives, handles curves, and shifts in response to changes in road conditions. During the first two weeks of your resolution, you're likely to encounter unanticipated obstacles, bumps in the road. Like the engine of a new car that knocks once it's on the highway, your resolution may need some tuning to get it humming on the open road. Fine-tuning your resolution in response to early experiences and new insight is part of the process of succeeding. Don't give up if your resolution doesn't prove to be an entirely smooth ride for the first couple of miles.

Albert Einstein famously once remarked, "In theory, theory and practice are the same. In practice, they are not." Like the scientist faced with an unexpected result, you may need to revisit some assumptions, but if your resolution adheres to rule 1—"A microresolution is *easy*"—then your resolution will be achievable with some tweaking. For example, if your resolution's cue is clock- or calendar-based, you may find that the day you picked isn't the best or that the hour you selected puts you in a squeeze. It's very common to adjust a schedule cue during the early days of a microresolution. What's important is that you find a better permanent spot, instead of deciding ad hoc that *right now is no good*. The day and time must become regular if your new behavior is to become part of autopilot.

One "easy" clock-based microresolution I made surprised me by requiring a lot of tuning to succeed—*to take a multivitamin first thing in the morning*. Sounds like a breeze, doesn't it? My intention was to take the vitamin before heading downstairs, since once I'm into cooking breakfast and packing lunch even something as simple as gulping down a vitamin becomes a lost cause. But taking that ginormous vitamin on an empty stomach proved so unappealing that I decided to switch to bedtime, which didn't work out any better. I had read that a pill taken before bed should be washed down with a full glass of water, and after a couple of sleeps interrupted by visits to the bathroom, I decided bedtime was a lousy bet, too. So I moved the vitamins to my workplace, intending to take them right after lunch. That fixed the timing issue, but I continued to tune, ultimately swapping out the horse pills for bigger but chewable ones that tasted like berries (well, kind of). The chewable vitamins were sweet, even clocking a couple of calories, so eating one after lunch was a poor man's treat, and the habit stuck. Not all resolutions are so tortured in their tuning, and I've taken on more complicated ones that took no detours at all. My point is simply that even a seemingly easy and straightforward resolution might require tuning to perfect, because you're trying to get it right for always and forever.

Linda began a microresolution to forgo the big hunk of bread that was served with soup at the San Francisco café she favored for her weekday lunch. The bread was delicious but rich in calories, and she was looking to work the vital margin to drop some weight and to stop leaning so heavily on simple carbohydrates in her daily diet. But almost immediately after making her resolution, she began shifting her lunch venue, freeing her from any lunchtime strictures. Since the framing and cue for her resolution had been menu specific, it didn't work as a guideline anywhere else. So Linda reframed her resolution to one that would work in virtually any eatery: *to choose a flourless lunch option*, meaning no bread, pasta, pizza, pretzels, or baked treats. Although now more broadly applicable, this resolution was still reasonable and limited, as it applied only to workday lunch. Now Linda hops from place to place using the tuned resolution as her guideline and finds she is eating healthier and more varied food, has lost weight, and feels better overall. Linda's husband, Andy, then took up a variant of her resolution, *no simple carbs after 3:00 p.m.*, and lost eight pounds in three months.

The test drive often reveals unanticipated obstacles that need to be addressed in order for a resolution to succeed. The first night I sent myself the message *It's really just as fast to hang it up* when I removed my coat, I responded by heading straight to the closet. Unfortunately, I found immediately that *it really isn't just as fast to hang it up* when the closet is already jammed with coats and has not a single free hanger. It took me a full minute to wrestle my coat into place next to the doublet costume my husband had worn playing Hamlet years ago. In order for my message to work, obviously, its premise had to be true: Hanging up my coat had to be *virtually* as fast as dropping it on a chair (and then hanging it up later). So I weeded out the closet, removing rarely worn items (*alas, poor doublet*) and adding a dozen new hangers, and then the message was able to work its magic. The closet situation wasn't new, but my resolution highlighted a systemic issue that had never before been addressed.

Building a new behavior exposes the systems you live by but never consciously designed. If you resolve to make your bed each day and it takes too long and comes out looking rumpled and lopsided, you may decide to replace a slippery coverlet and blankets with a comforter that speeds up bed making and produces a smoother result. If you resolve to get up on the first ring of the alarm rather than indulging in multiple snooze sessions, you may find that an alarm that slowly infuses the room with light before ringing is a gentler wake-up call than one that screams in the pitch dark of the early morning. Shaking up a routine with a microresolution exposes obstacles that subtly hindered past efforts to improve. That's why the test-drive period is crucial to success.

Although most tuning takes place in the early weeks of a new microresolution, you may find yourself tweaking months on. Remember my zero-tolerance resolution not to allow grooming products to clutter my bathroom countertop? I fanatically practiced this behavior until it was habit and then decided to dial it back a bit. There was really no point in putting away items at bedtime that would be needed first thing in the morning, so I allowed myself to leave these out overnight. This sped up the morning routine and didn't effectively disturb my goal of a neat bathroom, as the untidiness was literally kept in the dark. The tweak was made months after I had successfully established the habit of keeping the counter clear.

A microresolution should succeed every time. If you aren't succeeding, rethink, reframe, reschedule, and rescope your resolution until you can put a ring on it. If it seems like a cop-out to adjust your resolution after your initial commitment, it's not. The test drive is a period for gauging obstacles and confronting what you are willing or able to do to make progress. Scaling back is far better than quitting. As you gain experience in making microresolutions, you'll get smarter at predicting complications, framing for maximum effect, and identifying the best cues. Stick with your resolutions until they stick, and soon success itself will be a habit.

The Lesson of the Magic Rose Geranium

When I was growing up, my mother would sometimes buy me inexpensive storybooks at the supermarket to keep me happy while she shopped. A story in one of these books called, "The Magic Rose Geranium" became a great favorite of mine. As I remember it, the story is about a woman who lives in a house that has become very shabby. She is depressed by her surroundings, yet when she looks around at all there is to do, she feels overwhelmed and never makes a start.

One day an old friend comes to visit the woman and brings her a rose geranium as a gift. The geranium brings joy to the woman, but she suddenly sees how shabby her tablecloth looks next to the bright flowers, so she buys a new one. The tablecloth makes the rug look worn and gray, so she replaces it. The bright rug shows up the dinginess of the cupboards, so she paints them a fresh yellow. Each improvement the woman makes in her surroundings inspires another, until the entire house, even its yard and picket fence, are shipshape. The woman feels cheerful and energized all the time.

After putting the final touches on her house, the woman catches sight of her image in a mirror and sees herself clearly for the first time in years. Her hair is untidy, her clothes drab and in poor repair. Shocked by her appearance, the woman takes her newfound can-do spirit and applies it to her own person. Soon the woman is as well turned out and groomed as her now-tidy house.

When the friend who brought the geranium as a gift comes

to visit next, she can hardly believe her eyes and asks the woman how it was that after so many years of neglect she was able to transform her house and herself. The woman declares, "It's all thanks to that magic rose geranium!"

A microresolution operates like the magic rose geranium. Each successful resolution boosts your spirit, energy, and confidence, inspiring more progress. The key is simply to make a start.

MICRORESOLUTIONS IN ACTION

I t's time to apply what you learned in part 1 to making a micro-resolution in a specific area of self-improvement. Each one of the *rules* chapters used examples from different categories of personal development to illustrate a single microresolution principle at work; the chapters in part 2 pivot that perspective, each examining the utility of microresolutions through the lens of a single and popular area of self-improvement.

Remember as you take on a broader perspective: only two microresolutions at a time. Some of these microresolution success stories may seem so ingeniously simple that you believe they can be adopted wholesale, but don't be fooled. No matter how modest a shift in behavior, it must be pursued with rigor and single-minded purpose to succeed. A new habit takes hold only through consistent repetition, and that takes concentration and effort. Don't try to make a dozen microresolutions; instead prove to yourself you can succeed at *one*—pick a resolution and practice it relentlessly until it's on the path to true autopilot. Working one or two resolutions at a time, you'll make a lot of progress in just the first six months.

In sharing some of my own microresolution experiences I hope I'm not creating the impression that I have conquered every area of self-improvement or met all my personal goals. In several areas I've achieved results far beyond my expectations; in others I have made real progress; in some categories I have a long way to go. My aim in recounting my microresolution experiences and those of others is simply to provide some solid examples to inform your efforts, not to advocate for particular standards or lifestyle choices. *Small Move, Big Change* is about personal empowerment—not about *you should*, all about *how you can*.

The art of self-improvement is not about perfection but about priorities. To succeed in any endeavor one must assess and rank opportunities on an ongoing basis, and your self-improvement priorities will change as you change. You might begin by putting all your attention on fitness, make good progress, and then switch your attention to improving a relationship. You might find after making two microresolutions focused on organization, that what remains unreformed doesn't seem as important as tackling a different category, such as spending. Some targets may never make it off the bottom of your list because other prospects are always more compelling. Investing in continuous self-improvement means that there is no final item to be checked off the list.

Each section in part 2 is devoted to a different category of self-improvement. Not all of these may apply to you, of course, and you may be tempted to skip ahead to an area of particular interest or importance, but I recommend you start by reading the first chapter, "Sleep." Whatever self-improvement objectives drive your interest in this book, getting more rest will give a boost to your efforts and improve the quality of your life in ways you can't imagine.

CHAPTER 10

Sleep

> Sleep that knits up the ravell'd sleave of care,
> The death of each day's life, sore labour's bath,
> Balm of hurt minds, great nature's second course,
> Chief nourisher in life's feast.

> —William Shakespeare, *Macbeth*

If you're like most people living a modern life, you aren't getting enough sleep. You skimp on shut-eye throughout the week, chide yourself to get more rest, yet somehow rarely make it into bed in time to have a shot at the magic eight hours. Despite the devastating and well-documented effects of sleep deprivation—diminished strength, impaired reflexes, faulty decision making, flagging spirits—almost three-quarters of adults in the United States get less than six hours of sleep a night.*

For years I tried to force myself to bed at an earlier hour, but it wasn't until I began making microresolutions that I was able to crack my personal behavioral code and achieve a full night's

---

* Katherine Harmon, "How Slight Sleep Deprivation Could Add Extra Pounds," *Scientific American*, October 24, 2012.

sleep on a regular basis. Since my college days I had been a sleep cheater, burning the candle at both ends and counting on the adrenaline of work and responsibility to keep me going. When my energy flagged in the afternoon, I rebooted myself with sugary snacks alongside others fortifying themselves with carbs and caffeine. Once home from work, I made dinner, reviewed homework, attended to general household needs, and managed the protracted bedtime routine of my young daughter. By the time I had finished everything, I just wanted to flake out on the sofa in front of the TV with a glass of wine. This pitiful bacchanal usually didn't get under way until close to ten; since I had to get up at six, every moment I spent on that couch was a debit against a good night's sleep. Night after night I was getting to bed between midnight and 1:00 a.m., even on those nights when I felt beat by nine o'clock. As the week wore on, I became more and more tired.

Every year I tried to get more sleep simply by naming the hour I should be in bed, focusing on the result I wanted to achieve rather than examining the behavioral patterns that stood between me and a reasonable night's sleep. Once I discovered the microresolution, I realized that the key to getting to bed earlier wouldn't be watching the clock but reforming the habits that, taken in sum, kept me up later than I knew was wise. I decided to take a run at sleep the microresolution way: by closely observing my evening habits in order to identify a behavioral change that would translate into more sleep more often.

In thinking through a typical evening's events, I was struck by how often I fell asleep on the living room couch for an hour or more before finally going up to bed. Why was it that I couldn't get myself upstairs to bed even after it was clear that I was brain-dead? After paying special attention to this routine for a few evenings, I realized that once I entered a dozy state, I couldn't face performing the series of bedtime rites that stood between me and hitting the pillow. I couldn't imagine mustering the energy for tooth brushing, flossing, contact-lens maintenance, face washing, toning, moisturizing, medicating, pajama donning, and phone charging, so I mindlessly snoozed on the couch hoping to be blown upstairs by a second wind. Worse, after finally peeling myself off the couch, climbing the stairs, and performing my bedtime routine, I'd suddenly find myself wide awake from my "nap." Finally ready for bed, I no longer felt sleepy. Thinking about this sequence of events, I resolved:

> **To prepare myself for bed immediately after putting my daughter to sleep**

Rather than giving in to the almost irresistible impulse to charge down to the den as soon as I had put my daughter into bed, I instead completely prepared myself for sleep before diving onto the divan. Everything that I needed to do before retiring I did before heading downstairs, from flossing to phone charging. Thus when I began to snooze I could just rise up, zombielike, and lumber off to bed. Already nice and dozy and without a single thing to do before slipping between the sheets, I fell asleep almost instantaneously.

After some months I tuned my resolution so that I prepared for bed at the same time as my daughter, which gave me a bit more time to relax with my husband after my daughter's bedtime. I followed my *already-ready-for-bed* resolution with another resolution: *to have zero tolerance for recreational computer activity after 10:00 p.m,* because giving in to a sudden impulse to look something up or finally order that special stain remover often turned into a ninety-minute surfing session (and research shows that the brightness of the computer screen is itself revitalizing).* My two resolutions translated into at least ten hours more sleep per week, a game changer. I had vainly wagged the go-to-bed-earlier finger at myself for years, but once I began building targeted habits through microresolutions, I made sustainable progress.

If you carefully examine the actions leading up to bedtime, you'll be able to design a microresolution that reforms your behavior in a way that paves the way for improved sleep on a regular basis. And according to the latest research, a good sleep may turn out to be the essential ingredient in achieving personal goals.

Fatigue is the enemy of self-improvement. Bucking autopilot requires energy and focus, so sticking with a pledge to change is harder when you're weary. And it's when you are fatigued that you're most vulnerable to temptation and self-indulgence. In a research paper exploring why discipline yields to temptation, willpower researcher Roy Baumeister notes the powerful role sleep plays in restoring the self and how fatigue erodes self-control:

> The self's resources are restored during sleep and then become progressively depleted during the day, especially insofar as the day makes demands for choices and self-control. Hence failures of self-control are rare in the morning and become progressively more likely as the day wears on. Many patterns of self-control show these temporal patterns. Hardly anyone gets up and breaks a diet first thing in the morning, for example. Instead, it is late at night that one yields to temptation. Similar patterns are found for addictive relapse, alcohol indulgence, impulsive crimes, regrett-

---

* Laura Bell, "In Eyes, a Clock Callibrated by Wavelengths of Light," *The New York Times*, July 4, 2011.

able sexual indiscretions, and the like. . . . Impulsive purchasing behavior should become more and more likely as the day wears on, and sleep-deprived people should be most vulnerable to making them.*

A good night's sleep means a stronger ego with greater powers of concentration and self-control, exactly what's required to follow through with making a change in habitual behavior. Any self-improvement target will be easier to achieve if you regularly get a good night's sleep. New research shows that beyond generally fortifying your self-control, increasing sleep can give you an edge in some areas of self-improvement, particularly weight control.

Trying to lose weight while cheating on sleep is a near impossibility. Why? Because when you start the day depleted, you are likely to compensate for your lack of energy with a different kind of fuel, *food*. If you find yourself craving a carbohydrate-rich snack in the absence of hunger (i.e., pangs), what you're really after is an energy boost: You're not *hungry*, you're *tired*.

My own experiments with sleep and appetite aren't scientific, but they're consistent: The more regular my rest, the less junk food I crave and the easier it is for me to maintain my weight. The correlation between my afternoon cravings for carbs and rest is so tight that if I substitute a catnap for a Coffee Nip, I can kill off my desire for sugar for the rest of the day. Our continental cousins have the advantage here, as the midday break for lunch that many Spaniards, French, and Italians enjoy at home is long enough to allow for a nap, perhaps one reason that these rich countries haven't experienced the same obesity rates as the United States.

---

* Roy F. Baumeister, "Yielding to Temptation: Self-Control Failure, Impulsive Purchasing, and Consumer Behavior," *Journal of Consumer Research* 28, no. 4 (March 2002): 670–76.

New findings from sleep research confirm and go further than my personal observations. Two recent studies compared the daily caloric intake of study participants after 8-hour and 5.5-hour sleeps. Both studies found that following the nights of reduced sleep, participants consumed significantly more calories (five hundred calories on average for men),[*] mostly in snacks and carbohydrates.[†] Another study conducted at Stanford University[‡] found that weight and appetite are tightly correlated with sleeping habits. Subjects in the study who regularly slept less than eight hours a night had a higher body mass index (BMI) than those who generally slept eight or more hours. Moreover, each hour of lost sleep correlated exactly to an incremental rise in BMI; those with the highest BMIs slept the least. The study found that sleeping less than 7.7 hours a night caused a hormonal imbalance that led to increased appetite and reduced satisfaction, a lethal combination for any would-be dieter. If one of your goals is weight loss, a microresolution focused on sleep could be a turning point for you.

Current research findings support what most of us already know: Sleep is highly correlated with mood.[§] If you're constantly running in the red with sleep, exhaustion will make you feel, well, *exhausted* when it comes to grappling with life. When you're well rested, you're naturally more upbeat, optimistic, can-do. When you're worn out, you're more easily confused and simple tasks become harder, chipping away at your confidence. And it's when

[*] L. Brondel et al., "Acute Sleep Deprivation Increases Food Intake in Healthy Men," *American Journal of Clinical Nutrition* 91 (2010): 1550–59.

[†] R. Leproult, E. Van Couter, "Role of Sleep and Sleep Loss in Hormonal Release and Metabolism," *Pediatric Neuroendocrinology* 17 (2010): 11–21.

[‡] S. Taheri et al., "Short Sleep Duration Is Associated with Reduced Leptin, Elevated Ghrelin, and Increased Body Mass Index." *Public Library of Science Medicine* 1, no. 3 (December 2004): e62.

[§] C. Mah, "Extended Sleep and the Effects on Mood and Athletic Performance in Collegiate Swimmers," Annual Meeting of the Associated Professional Sleep Societies, June 9, 2008.

we're beat that we're most likely to be irritable, snapping at a child or blowing up at a coworker. If one of your goals is improving a relationship, your work performance, or self-confidence, increasing sleeping hours can give your efforts a real boost.

People spend a fortune on antiaging creams and cosmetics to firm and refresh the skin; sleep does a better job of rejuvenation, and it's *free*! The old notion of "beauty sleep" was validated in a 2010 study conducted in Sweden,* where independent raters assessed photographs of people before and after sleep deprivation. Researchers found that people deprived of sleep appeared "less healthy, less attractive, and more tired compared with when they are well rested." If one of your goals is to improve your appearance through exercise, dieting, or better grooming, not only will logging some extra ZZZs help you by strengthening your concentration and self-control, but also you'll immediately be better looking!

Three studies conducted by the Stanford Sleep Disorders Clinic and Research Laboratory at Stanford University found that getting more sleep significantly improved athletic performance. When Stanford's swimming, basketball, and women's tennis teams increased their sleep to ten hours a night for six or seven weeks, they showed marked and measurable improvement in performance: swimming faster,† sinking more baskets,‡ hitting and serving more accurately.§ All three studies reported that the athletes enjoyed elevated mood, greater vigor, and lower levels of fatigue after

---

* J. Axelisson, et al., "Beauty Sleep: Experimental Study on the Perceived Health and Attractiveness of Sleep Deprived People," *BMJ* 2010, 341:c6614.

† Mah, "Extended Sleep and the Effects on Mood and Athletic Performance in Collegiate Swimmers," study results presented at the 22nd annual meeting for the Associated Professional Sleep Societies, June 9, 2008.

‡ C. D. Mah et al., "The Effects of Sleep Extension on the Athletic Performance of Collegiate Basketball Players," *Sleep* 34, no. 7 (2011): 943–50.

§ C. Mah, "Study Shows Sleep Extension Improves Athletic Performance and Mood," study results presented at the 23rd Annual Meeting of the Associated Professional Sleep Societies, June 8, 2009.

extending their sleeping hours. The research prompted Mark Remy of *Runner's World* to comment that perhaps competitors should consider engaging in "sleep-loading" before a race to achieve an edge.* If fitness is one of your goals, starting with a microresolution that helps you get to bed earlier could improve your performance and give you the energy you need to stick with a fitness program.

If only people understood the magical and irreplaceable value of sleep, pledges to get more of it would headline the "top ten resolutions" lists each year. Sleep is fuel—fuel for your brain, body, and spirit—and microresolutions can help you get more of it.

Winning the Battle for More Sleep Through Microresolutions

In order to craft a microresolution that helps get you to bed earlier, begin by asking yourself what it is that keeps you from the sheep. When you feel yourself fading out, why don't you go to bed? It might be extra work, a special occasion, or a big night out. But most of the time we put off bedtime in order to wring more leisure hours from an ordinary day. Between work and other responsibilities, going to bed early puts a damper on the already precious commodity known as *time off*. We don't feel like heading straight to bed as soon as our work and household chores are done, unlike the days of old when lack of heat and light drove people under the covers as soon as it grew dark. *At last*, we exult, finishing our final chore, *it's time to relax and have fun!* We stretch our waking hours to the max in order to enjoy greater leisure. But there's nothing fun about being tired all the

---

* Mark Remy, "Forget Carbs, Try Sleep-Loading," Remy's World, *Runner's World*, June 15, 2009.

time—it's stressful, not relaxing. And whatever bonus leisure time we gain by cheating on sleep all week gets wiped out by lying in bed until noon on Saturday. Many of us operate at half throttle the entire weekend as we struggle to catch up, just in time to begin all over again on Monday night. But if you manage to regularize your sleep through microresolutions, your energy and mood will burn steady every day and your weekend hours will be more enjoyable and productive.

Cookie Monsters

Falling asleep on the couch is one cue that you should pack it in; another is a late-night impulse to raid the cookie jar. Although Neil had to get up before 7:00 a.m., he often stayed up past midnight, usually watching television or spending time on the Internet. Every night around ten o'clock, he would get a craving for a treat and go in search of a sweet snack. He found the desire for something sugary at that hour overwhelming even though he had eaten dinner only a couple of hours earlier, was still full, and needed to lose twenty pounds. Observing his late-night routine closely with the aim of identifying a behavior he might target to get to bed earlier, Neil realized that the late-night snack wasn't simply a ritual treat causing him to gain weight, but a stratagem for staving off drowsiness. As much as he enjoyed his leisure activities at night, realizing that his late-night eating was causing him both to gain weight and lose sleep led Neil to rethink the value he placed on recreational TV and computer time.

Neil made a microresolution *not to snack to stay awake.* The framing was very canny; it didn't dictate a bedtime or prohibit snacking to address true hunger, it just prohibited using food as a crutch to stay awake. A desire for sweets in the absence of hunger pangs meant no snack; if he was too tired to stay up without a stimulant, he went to bed. Neil began turning in earlier and over a couple of months dropped several pounds by skipping the fridge raid in the final hour before bed. "I was amazed," he says, "at how soon after I began craving a sweet snack I ended up going to bed. I never realized how tired I really was until I stopped eating late at night."

Such "pick-me-ups" are exactly what you should avoid when you begin to fade out in the evening. In a study conducted at Northwestern University on how the timing of meals influences weight gain, researchers found that mice fed identical diets at different times had strikingly different weight outcomes. Mice who ate during their natural sleeping hours gained 28 percent more weight than control mice eating during waking hours.[*] When you eat a bowl of ice cream at 10:30 p.m., you're eating during your natural sleeping hours—is the last half hour of *American Idol* really worth it?

Getting It All In

One way to increase leisure hours without skimping on sleep is to get evening routines started or finished up more quickly. Depending on how much flexibility you have, you might well be able to complete some routines (such as dinner) sixty minutes sooner, giving you more time to spend on kicking back or accomplishing tasks before bed. Jacqueline got her kids to make a microresolution to unload the dishwasher before she came home from work, making cleaning up from dinner faster; Betsy moved her gym sessions from after work to her lunch hour; Jeff

---

[*] D. M. Arble, J. Bass, A. D. Laposky, M. H. Viterna, F. W. Turek, "Circadian Timing of Food Intake Contributes to Weight Gain," *Obesity* 17, no. 11 (November 2009): 2100–211.

shortened his regular weekday dinners by making a resolution to drop his usual round of coffee and dessert, which also helped with his weight-loss goals. Again, your resolutions for creating more leisure time will be personal to your habits and circumstances. If you make dinner in the evening, you'll create resolutions that are entirely different from those of someone who regularly goes to the gym in the evening and grabs dinner on the way home. But if you can focus a resolution on organizing an activity so that it uses up less evening time, you'll have a better chance of hitting the hay at an earlier hour.

Prime-Time Sleep

The hypnotic and calming effect of television often keeps us up past bedtime, chipping away at precious shut-eye. We intend to pack it in at the end of our show, but once it's over, we decide to watch a few minutes of the next program—intending just to see the monologue of a late-night talk show or the lead story on the late news. Lured into the next TV cycle, we settle into the show without ever really making a conscious decision to trade entertainment for sleep. Television networks are expert at keeping viewers in their seats with program teasers and shows that open with a bang. The network cues you to keep watching, just as the links on a Web page cue you to keep surfing.

Deborah often went to bed at midnight, even though she had to get up at 6:30 on weekday mornings and her target bedtime was 10:30 p.m. As the week wore on, she became more and more tired, and she often slept until eleven on Saturday morning. Tired of showing up for work exhausted nearly every day, she began thinking through the underlying causes of her going to bed later than she intended. Noting that television was usually what kept her from her bed's embrace, she considered how she might take more control of her television-viewing habits in order to get more sleep during the week. Deborah made a microresolution *to watch only prerecorded television on weeknights*. Recording shows allowed her to view a late-night program at a more reasonable hour and to watch long programs over two nights rather than staying up late on airing night to see the end. Even a show with an early broadcast hour was better prerecorded, Deborah discovered, as it allowed her to fast-forward through the ads, saving at least twenty minutes per hour of television. Because her microresolution forced her to deliberately choose and record her weekday shows in advance, she no longer fell prey to network come-ons to continue watching past her bedtime.

Recording programs takes the "event" excitement out of a TV show (*it's starting! it's on!*), so Deborah had to get used to thinking in terms of an entertainment bank to draw on rather than a schedule (*tonight's a really good night!*). But once she took control of her evening schedule back from *TV Guide*, she found herself getting to bed, on average, an hour earlier. By recording all her shows, she disrupted the real-time cues that kept her watching more and sleeping less.

Swapping prime-time television for prime-time sleep proved to be a winning trade. Deborah says she is more productive at work, is happier, and has more leisure weekend hours since she no longer needs to catch up on sleep Saturday morning.

Morning Glory

Going to bed earlier is one way to up your shut-eye; the other option is sleeping longer on the morning end. If you develop prep routines for the night before, you can get up later and still make the early bus.

Take the tried-and-true strategy of preparing work clothes the night before. Laying out every item you'll be wearing tomorrow will allow you to spend more time in bed in the morning, and you may even sleep more peacefully knowing that all you have to do when you wake up is shower and step into your clothes. Eliminating sartorial fumbling in the morning speeds things along and takes the stress out of getting ready. Why do so many of us resist adopting this habit when it is so straightforward and provides such an obvious benefit? Well, because you have to give it some precious evening time, because it's boring, because you don't want to think about preparing for the next day once you start to relax at home, and you haven't built a technique to make the exercise of this behavior mindless and quick. But once you find the right slot for this activity (perhaps when you change out of your work clothes) and drill it faithfully, it will begin to work its way into autopilot.

Your first microresolution doesn't have to nail preparing the whole outfit; its action could be focused solely on selecting a shirt and tie or finding run-free stockings and a matching pair of shoes. The greater speed and ease you experience in dressing due to the elements you have prepared will affect your mindset and over time likely lead to your resolution to organize the entire outfit the night before.

It's worth repeating that you'll very likely experience internal resistance to performing a new behavior pattern. Practicing old routines is comforting, and building new routines is stressful because the new behavior requires concentration and willpower and an old behavior doesn't. That's why even "easy" resolutions can still feel like a heavy lift.

What discretionary activities keep you up too late to get a good night's sleep? Reading just one more chapter? Internet browsing? Television? Phone, text, or chat sessions? Suddenly remembering work, homework, or tasks that must be completed by morning? Scrutinize your evening and morning routines and see what you might resolve to do differently to tip the balance in the direction of more sleep.

Sleep is so undervalued in our workaholic culture it's like a secret weapon for those who appreciate the advantages it offers. In writing this book, I was often struck by my erratic productivity. Some days would pass with so little progress that I would lose confidence in my ability to finish on time or realize my ambitions for the book. On other days I would be hugely productive and feel upbeat about the book's prospects. Soon a pattern became clear: The really good days nearly always followed a longer night's sleep. So I added a microresolution message to the mix of sleep resolutions I had already made. When tempted to stay up to complete a task, watch a show, finish reading a novel, or even work on the book, I would remind myself, *I'm more successful when I get more sleep.*

Sleep is the secret sauce of waking hours, of living. Your whole quality of life will improve if you get more of it. Life is something to rest up for.

CHAPTER 11

Fitness

> Lack of activity destroys the good condition of every human being.
>
> —Plato

P ledges to hit the gym are right up at the top of the most popular annual resolution lists, representing the collective desire to get and stay fit. I won't bother to recount at length why our lives, even fifty years ago, were more active than they are today. I'm sure you can check the boxes—fewer conveniences, more active jobs, more walking and cycling, physically demanding chores. In many parts of the world, physical exertion in the service of survival is still a dawn-to-dusk affair. For someone working sixteen hours in the fields, the notion of heading to the gym after work must seem bizarre indeed. But for many in the developed world, fitness has mostly become *fit-in-ness*, trying to cram in a bit of exercise to help compensate for all the inactive hours in the day.

Recent studies expose the damage done to health by our sedentary culture. Sitting at a desk by day and on a couch by night doesn't just contribute to weight gain; sitting is, literally, *a killer*.

It's not just that sitting causes our metabolic rate to plummet to a single calorie a minute, helping us to pile on the pounds; new research shows that our life span is shortened in direct proportion to the amount of time we sit each day. In a 2011 article entitled "Is Sitting a Lethal Activity?" the *New York Times* reported the dangerous consequences of sitting too much:

> Alpa Patel, an epidemiologist at the American Cancer Society, tracked the health of 123,000 Americans between 1992 and 2006. The men in the study who spent six hours or more per day of their leisure time sitting had an overall death rate that was about 20 percent higher than the men who sat for three hours or less. The death rate for women who sat for more than six hours a day was about 40 percent higher. Patel estimates that on average, people who sit too much shave a few years off of their lives.
>
> Another study, published last year in the journal *Circulation*, looked at nearly 9,000 Australians and found that for each additional hour of television a person sat and watched per day, the risk of dying rose by 11 percent.*

In the same *Times* article, Dr. James Levine of the Mayo Clinic likened an hourlong workout after a day of sitting to a smoker trying to undo the day's lung damage through an hour of jogging. "Excessive sitting," said Dr. Levine, "is a lethal activity."

But the *Times* article also contained some good news: It doesn't take a lot of activity to lower the health risks caused by

---

* James Vlahos, "Is Sitting a Lethal Activity?" *New York Times*, April 14, 2011.

inactivity. In a research study investigating why some people gain more than others on the same caloric allowance, Dr. Levine and his team found that small amounts of activity made the difference. Those who got up out of their seats every twenty minutes to walk around for two minutes were able to maintain steady blood-sugar and insulin levels, critical to weight loss and preventing illnesses such as diabetes, heart disease, and, according to some new research, cancer.

Another study, at the University of Minnesota, demonstrated that people who stand instead of sit while they work burn hundreds more calories per day.* Don Callahan, whom I knew as the chief administrative officer at Morgan Stanley before his move to Citibank, was the first person I knew to use a standing desk in his office to break up the hours of sitting while working. Now there are several companies working to redesign office furniture so that workers can stand or exercise as they work.

What these studies suggest is that small changes in behavior *at the margin* can result in significant health and fitness gains. So often our resolutions to get fit begin with ambitious pledges to visit the gym several times a week and end in reversion to complete inactivity a few weeks later. These *all-or-nothing* propositions demonstrate that we suffer not just from sedentariness but also from a complete lack of imagination when it comes to building fitness into our lives. We compartmentalize physical activity, thinking of it as something that happens "after work," "at the gym," or "on the tennis court," rather than developing a fitness mentality that instinctively keeps us moving and maximizes physical life at every opportunity.

If you've been meaning to start an ambitious fitness routine

---

* C. Reiff, K. Marlatt, D. R. Dengel, "Difference in Caloric Expenditure in Sitting Versus Standing Desks," *Journal of Physical Activity and Health* 9 (2012): 1009–16.

but just haven't been able to follow through, why not begin with a microresolution that breaks up the hours of sitting you do each day, such as getting up out of your seat at work every half hour and going to get a drink from the watercooler (movement with a hydration benefit). How about a resolution to stand one or two days a week during your bus or train commute, even when there is a seat available? Perhaps a microresolution to break up long hours of TV watching by doing jumping jacks or going up and down a flight of stairs during the commercials? What about carrying groceries instead of having them delivered or playing catch or Wii with your kid for ten minutes a day (more fitness, more bonding)?

Any change you make that keeps you off your keister will deliver health benefits and help transform a sedentary mindset into an active one. Small changes in activity will up your metabolism, contribute to steady blood sugar, and help mitigate the ill effects of a sedentary job. Such resolutions are worth making even if you already have a solid fitness routine, such as regularly going to the gym or riding your bike to work. The more you can interrupt long stretches of sitting to keep your body active, the better off you'll be in terms of overall fitness, alertness, health, and weight. The point is that any increase in activity has a positive fitness impact. And as the following microresolution examples show, building new physical activity into your day can be easy and rewarding.

Stair Master

Marissa had always been active in college, walking to campus, climbing stairs, and playing sports. But although she remained reasonably fit, she had little opportunity to move around at the office, where the demands of work kept her in her cube most of the day. Marissa worked in an office building with sixteen floors, and her first fitness microresolution was to take the stairs to meetings and the cafeteria in her building. Her office was on the fourteenth floor, ten floors above the cafeteria, so at a minimum (hitting the cafeteria once) she climbed twenty flights of stairs daily. At first Marissa had to stop and rest several times on the way back up the twenty flights to her office, but after a week or so, she found she was able to charge right up. She lost four pounds and some inches and gained in overall stamina, all from a single change in office habit. (It's important to point out that Marissa was fit enough that this resolution qualified as *easy*; if you're very out of shape, you might start with two flights of stairs in each direction.)

An overweight person who makes no other changes to his diet and fitness routine can lose over ten pounds in a year by climbing two flights of stairs a day. According to researchers at the University of Pennsylvania School of Medicine,* climbing stairs burns far more calories per minute than tennis, swimming, racquetball, cycling, swimming, running, or walking. Regular stair climbing can have a profound effect on fitness level and cardiovascular health. If your workplace or home has stairs, consider leveraging this resource in your next fitness resolution.

From Fat to Fit in Four Minutes

After years of inactivity, Hannah made a microresolution to jog in place for four minutes every morning before breakfast. At first the four minutes seemed more like fifteen, and she was tired long before the timer went off. But because her resolution

---

* M. S. Dolan et al., "'Take the Stairs Instead of the Escalator': Effect of Environmental Prompts on Community Stair Use and Implications for a National 'Small Steps' Campaign," *Obesity Reviews* 7, no. 1 (February 2006): 25–32.

was limited and reasonable, she stuck with it rather than face that she was unable to exercise for even four minutes a day. After a few weeks of the new routine the four-minute jog was more boring than tiring, so Hannah took her jog outside, making a circuit of a few blocks. After several months the four-minute jog had on most days turned into a thirty-minute run to a nearby beach. It was so lovely to find herself at the beach early in the morning that Hannah began adding a quick ocean dip even in cold weather (the beach was populated with Russian immigrants who swim all through winter, and Hannah is very competitive). She went on to lose nearly forty pounds, and her first resolution had been simply to run in place for four minutes every day. *Work the margin.*

Tennis, Anyone?

If you've been very active in the past and have been meaning to begin a new fitness routine, you might have a harder time limiting your resolution to the strictly reasonable. Remembering the glory days of running for miles, swimming scores of laps, or pumping big iron can make a modest resolution seem like conceding defeat, but that's the wrong mindset. Whatever you manage to build into your routine now enhances both your health and your chances of reaching more ambitious fitness objectives in the future.

Orin had an extremely active youth, playing competitive baseball and tennis, but he became an academic, lost the habit of regular exercise, and fell out of shape. Year after year, his New Year's resolution was to return to tennis and play several times a week, but he was never able to sustain his resolution beyond the first few sessions. His rusty skills, a shoulder injury, the difficulty of finding a regular partner, and the hassle of booking courts frustrated his attempts to return to regular play, yet he stayed fixed on tennis as his ideal fitness routine. But when his young family adopted a dog, Orin began taking her for a short walk every evening and immediately began to feel better physically. Building on his new habit, Orin made a microresolution to take a longer dog walk on Fridays after work. The walk was substantial, a couple of miles on a trail near his home, taking about an hour to complete. He was often tempted to bag the walk in favor of working longer or going for a drink with a friend at the week's end, but he kept faith with his "no excuses" resolution.

Orin was surprised by the benefits the longer weekly walk generated. Following the walk, he snacked less, slept better, awoke fresher, and over the first eight weeks lost four pounds. Most surprising, he found that the enforced solitude and break from the computer screen allowed him to think through difficult portions of his writing, and he returned to work with greater motivation.* Dogs, those super creatures of habit, are born cues for walking resolutions—as soon as Orin came home on Friday, the dog would leap about in anticipation of their special excursion. The dog's joyful physicality was catching, and over time Orin found himself making the long walk two or more times a week, although his sole commitment remained the Friday walk.

Success Is Showing Up

Despite maintaining a gym membership for several years, Lindsay's annual resolution *to get fit* was usually kaput by

---

* "All truly great thoughts are conceived while walking."—Friedrich Nietzsche, *Twilight of the Idols*.

mid-February. Each year she was determined to succeed, but every year her willpower collapsed after a few weeks of struggling to complete her training circuit or follow through with a class. Lindsay would anticipate her gym session all day at work and then at the last minute find a reason to avoid her commitment.

But after having some success with microresolutions in other areas, she decided to take a different approach to the gym. Rather than pledging to go each night after work as she had in the past, Lindsay resolved *to go to the gym on Monday nights and row for fifteen minutes.* In reducing her exercise commitment by such a large degree, she shifted the entire focus of her resolution from performing an hour of grueling exercise to simply getting to the gym and changing up. Showing up, Lindsay discovered, was the entire psychological battle. By absolutely establishing her Monday-night gym habit, she learned from practical experience how to best advance her fitness goals. Lindsay switched to a gym near her apartment instead of one near work, so that she could avoid showering and changing back into her work clothes before heading home, saving herself at least half an hour of evening time. When she next added to her routine, she added a morning session on a day when she didn't need to get to work until nine o'clock, and she later added a session before brunch on Saturday, so that she had only one late night a week. Lindsay established different exercise routines for different sessions, alternating among rowing, biking, and the elliptical climber so that she didn't get bored. After so many failed attempts to build a gym habit, within a year of her first microresolution Lindsay was fit and relishing life as a gym rat.

How I Found My Way Back to Fitness Through Microresolutions

During my twenties I always exercised. There was my *go for the burn* video era; the period during which I ran twice around the reservoir in New York's Central Park each day, until I injured my foot; my swim-a-mile-a-day period; and then the era of working a Nautilus circuit while listening to a Walkman (back in the day!). Once I went to work on Wall Street, I let my gym membership lapse, but by then I had a dog who got me up and moving early on an hourlong walk in all weather before I left for the office. I worked upward of eighty hours a week programming, sitting hour after hour, and getting up only to move around during compile time (usually to visit the M&M's machine on a colleague's desk). My ambition to excel at work outpaced my ambition to be fit, I fell out of shape, and my weight climbed. My dog got old and the two-mile walk became two blocks, and then my dog died. All my efforts to get back to the gym were failures, even though there was a free gym at work. I would block time off in my calendar for a workout and instead just obsessively keep coding.

Finally, in my microresolution era, I took action. I resolved to see a personal trainer once a week in the office gym. When the trainer tested my fitness level, I could do only eleven sit-ups. The first few sessions were humiliating and left me with such sore muscles that I could barely lower myself into a chair. But I stuck with my limited and reasonable resolution, and I made steady progress. After establishing my weekly training session as a habit, I added an additional day at the gym and a day of walking to work.

For most of my exercising life, *buff* had been my goal and health an incidental benefit. When I began exercising again with a trainer, I had my eye on a closetful of clothes I couldn't fit into. But a strange thing happened on the way to skinny jeans—I discovered the pleasures of strength. That summer I vacationed with my parents and served as their stevedore, heaving their overpacked luggage pieces into airplane overheads, on and off trains, and into car trunks. Unlike the summer before, when my neck and shoulders were still sore days after arrival, after a year of limited workouts I suffered not a single ache. For the first time I felt more excited about being strong than about being slim. Strength, flexibility, and posture became my goals, and becoming trimmer simply a bonus. These days I walk every weekday for forty minutes and go to Pilates three times a week, and it all started with that half hour of personal training I resolved to honor every week.

Overreaching on fitness pledges is endemic in classic resolution-think. Inactive all year, we abruptly pledge to go to the gym every night after work, trying to blow away our inertia and dispel our self-disgust with a single, unrealistic promise. We imagine ourselves becoming trim and fit, but our fantasy doesn't include schlepping to the gym after a tiring day, toting and washing gym clothes, suiting up, struggling with simple exercise routines, the tedium of showering and blow-drying when we long to be on our way, or the unpleasantness of changing back into tired work clothes for the late commute home. If you struggle to make it to the gym at all, why would you suddenly pledge to yourself to make it to the gym five (or three or two) nights a week? Would you make such a promise to a friend? Would you call up a close pal and say, "Hey, I'll meet you every night at the gym to work out. It'll be great! No, no, I'm absolutely sure I can make it; cancel all your plans!" You wouldn't make such an ill-considered promise, because we generally don't treat a friend's aspirations and commitment as cavalierly as we treat our own. *Small Move, Big Change* is about learning to honor the promises you make yourself as faithfully as you honor the important promises you make to others, and that means making only pledges you know you can keep and giving them your full commitment until they succeed.

Wherever you are in your fitness goals, whether you're adding to an established program or just trying to get started, the most important thing is to advance from where you are by making a realistic resolution you can follow through with and build from there. And if you aren't getting enough rest, start with a resolution that helps you get more sleep, because it's hard to honor an exercise commitment (even a reasonable one) when you're exhausted.

CHAPTER 12

Diet and Nutrition

Two elderly women are at a Catskill mountain resort,
and one of 'em says, "Boy, the food at this place is really
terrible." The other one says, "Yeah, I know; and such
small portions!"

—Woody Allen in *Annie Hall*

Losing weight tops the list of New Year's resolutions every
year, the most made, the most broken, the most likely to
be repeated when the next year rolls around. Yet diets
work; if you reduce the number of calories you consume, you'll
lose weight; it's simple chemistry. So why do most diet resolutions fail?

Eating is a complex set of behaviors and attitudes that runs
mostly on (*drum roll*) autopilot. Our eating habits are largely
unconscious, whether we are mindlessly nibbling off a friend's
plate or popping peanuts at a bar. In contrast to the unconscious
autopilot behaviors that drive our everyday eating, dieting requires that we be conscious of every morsel, weigh every food
option, and make endless choices. Making decisions at every

meal exhausts our self-control,* making it difficult to stick with most diets beyond the first few weeks. Additionally, our narrow concentration on *how much* we eat, measured in calories or carbohydrates, ignores other autopilot behaviors that determine satisfaction and success: *how* we eat, *why* we eat, *where* we eat, *what* we eat, *when* we eat, and how long we sleep.

One reason that prepackaged diets, liquid meals, cleanses, and other highly prescriptive diets have gained in popularity is because such diets become a new kind of autopilot. We don't need to think and decide; we just mindlessly consume what's in the package and our weight declines. Yet sooner or later we must return to eating in the real world, making daily decisions at the grocery store, cocktail party, movie snack bar, and cafeteria. It's then that our old eating habits reassert themselves, methodically undoing the progress we have made.

Every marginal change in behavior you make must be sustainable. Losing two pounds is a success if you keep it off for life; losing fifteen pounds is a failure if you gain it back in a year. Any shift in behavior you resolve to make must be one you are able to maintain: *Don't make resolutions you can't keep.*

Losing weight permanently means eating less for life. The only way to succeed at eating less for life is to *be satisfied with less.* Each of our eating behaviors——not just what and how much we eat—plays a critical role in satisfaction and in curbing the impulse to overeat. Reducing the microresolutions way doesn't require endless decisions, an abacus, or an app; the focus is on making discrete and permanent behavioral changes that reform autopilot so that it can maintain a healthy weight without mental effort.

---

* Kathleen D. Vohs, "Making Choices Impairs Subsequent Self-Control: A Limited-Resource Account of Decision Making, Self-Regulation, and Active Initiative," *Journal of Personality and Social Psychology* 94, no. 5 (May 2008): 883–98.

After years of failed diets, I've finally achieved *satisfied with less* through microresolutions. I've reached a kind of nirvana where I enjoy everything I eat more, feel satisfied, and can maintain my weight at a level that pleases me, about twenty-two pounds less than before I began modifying my eating habits through microresolutions. Before achieving *satisfied with less*, I treated myself to extra snacks and second portions but often felt unsatisfied. I would eat for energy and end up feeling sluggish. I would swear off sweets and end up bingeing on them. By targeting specific behaviors and attitudes for reform, I increased my eating satisfaction, upped my energy, consumed fewer calories, lost weight, and improved my health.

The three sections that follow ("The Engine," "Mindful Eating," and "Less") provide a framework for identifying a personal behavioral change at the vital margin that will advance a goal of eating more healthfully, with greater pleasure, while losing weight. You may be so used to adopting drastic tactics to lose weight that isolating one or two behavioral targets for reform takes some thought. The discussions below will help you sharpen your personal observations and zero in on a microresolution that will have an immediate and lasting impact. But remember: only two resolutions at a time.

The Engine

Your body is an engine that combusts nutrients and turns them into energy. An efficient and vigorous engine is essential to eating satisfaction and maintenance of a healthy weight. When your engine is running at peak, it demands nutrient-rich food, signals hunger at mealtimes, and doesn't crave excessive sweets, fats, and salts. An engine running at peak keeps up a stable burn that provides energy throughout the day, steadies mood, and contributes to a good sleep. In contrast, a body engine running suboptimally is always wanting, literally. It runs erratically, demanding fuel between meals, is prone to slumps and mood swings, and generates cravings and urges to binge. If your diet is poor, your sleep is inadequate, and you sit all day, your engine won't get many miles to the gallon. Rather than rushing to lose weight, first consider microresolutions designed to get your engine humming.

Sleep

As discussed at length in chapter 10, "Sleep," your engine can't run at peak without adequate rest. Following a night of poor sleep, your metabolism will run sluggishly, you may be plagued by cravings and hunger pangs, and you'll end up relying on carbohydrate-rich snacks to restore your energy when the inevitable slump arrives.

Replacing lost sleep with food is a sucker's trade. While adequate sleep will sustain you the entire day, whatever sugary snack you substitute for it will give you only a short burst of energy, leading you to refuel multiple times between meals. When you eat because you're tired rather than hungry, you're using food as a stimulant, a drug. That draggy feeling you experience mid-afternoon is better cured by more sleep, not more dessert.

When I first visited Google in connection with building the auction system for the company's innovative IPO, I was struck by the nifty lounge areas Google had set up for its employees. The free snack bars were stocked mostly with sugary treats—cookies and candies—and a few healthier options. When I visited a couple of years later in connection with building a transferable-employee-stock-option exchange for Googlers, most of the sweet treats had been banished and in their place was a host of healthy and delicious snack options. But something new had also been added to the mix—*napping pods* where tired programmers could crash for an hour during the day. While no official connection was made between the snack-bar changes and the napping pods, perhaps there was an implicit message—*sleep is a better fuel than sugar*. (I have to give a shout-out here to the Google cafeteria, known by those who are lucky enough to work or visit there as the best restaurant in town. Wonderful chefs whip up healthy global cuisine, often seasoned with herbs grown on the Google campus. Whenever we could, my team scheduled our meetings with Google close to noon so that our sessions could end with a visit to the cafeteria. My favorite station: "Namaste.")

How often do you get up to eat something while watching television late at night? Why not just go to sleep instead? It's madness to snack at night in order to stay awake unless forced to by a workload that can't be managed any other way. Late-night snacking interrupts the digestion that began after dinner, giving your body a new load to process just before sleep. New research demonstrates that eating late at night is more likely to cause weight gain than eating earlier in the day. If you have the habit of snacking between dinner and bedtime, you might want to focus your first diet microresolution on limiting or eliminating this behavior. See chapter 10 for a complete discussion of recent research, sleep's benefits, its relationship to weight, and some examples of microresolutions aimed at eliminating chronic sleep deprivation.

Stoking the Engine

Oscar Wilde famously wrote that a cynic "knows the price of everything and the value of nothing," and it might be said that the inveterate dieter knows the calorie count of everything and the nutritional value of nothing. Years of measuring foods in calories—whereby a couple of mini candy bars are equal to an apple—has led many to eat poorly in pursuit of eating less. Whatever your weight-loss goals, they will be more achievable if you feed yourself nutrient-rich food: lots of whole fruits and vegetables; legumes and grains; lean protein; adequate dairy for gender and age. Think of these foods as a nutritional baseline. We all have favorite foods that aren't of the highest nutrient value, but these should be eaten on top—not in place—of baseline foods. You don't need a degree in nutrition to know that there is no sane health scale where candy is the equal of fruit.

If your diet is poor, consider starting with microresolutions that focus on nutrition first, perhaps before you try to reduce what you're eating. If you're eating a crappy diet and you decide just to eat less of it, you'll be setting yourself up for failure, since the food you eat makes you prone to cravings, slumps, and binges. For example, if your diet is high in processed foods (pretzels, chips, baked goods, and the like) and low in whole foods (fruits, vegetables, whole grains), consider a microresolution to add some whole foods to your diet daily. A microresolution *to eat two whole fruits a day* will immediately improve your nutrition profile and give your engine a boost. If your breakfast is a nutritional bust (Pop-Tarts, Danish, commercial cereals, bagels, muffins, white toast), a microresolution to consume whole-grain cereal for breakfast would be a radical and positive nutritional change that could give you greater energy, alertness, health. If your dinner is meat heavy and vegetable light, doubling or tripling your green and root vegetables would be a huge health bonus. Sooner or later you'll need to reduce what you eat overall to lose weight, but getting your engine fired up and learning to appreciate whole foods alongside the other foods you love is a great place to start. Give your body engine high-octane food, real meals, and get it humming before you try to cut back. Reforming breakfast is the most powerful way to get your engine stoked and to begin to feel the difference between being *fed* and being *nourished*.

First Things First

Everyone learns at some point that breakfast is the most important meal of the day, but many folks on the go give it short shrift. A flimsy bowl of cereal, a white-bread bagel, a doughnut, a sugary muffin, or just coffee with milk is how many choose to start their day. Focusing a microresolution on improving breakfast is a great way to get on the road to *satisfied with less*.

"But I'm not hungry in the morning. Why waste my calories?" you might ask. Perhaps you aren't hungry for breakfast because between dinner and bedtime you ate (or drank) a fourth meal's worth of calories while watching television. Making a microresolution not to eat after dinner ensures that you'll arrive at breakfast with such good appetite that you'll find it almost unbearably satisfying.

If you stop eating at a reasonable hour in the evening, by breakfast the next morning you'll have gone ten to twelve hours without food, basically a fast (*break-fast*). With all the nutrients from the previous day now fully digested, your engine is primed to burn new fuel efficiently, so resolve to stoke it with something good. What you eat should give you energy until lunch without a midmorning slump.

Breakfast of Champions

Richard's morning routine was erratic and his breakfast often nutritionally poor. He generally grabbed a muffin or bagel on the way to work, the hour depending on his changing work schedule. Richard often felt hungry long before lunch and kept himself going with caffeine and the stray doughnut left by the coffee machine. His first dieting microresolution was simply *to eat breakfast at home on weekdays*. He felt that once he had left the house and was in a rush, he had little control over breakfast choices.

Eating breakfast at home forced Richard to think about and plan his meal, something he had never done when grabbing breakfast en route. His resolution had the extra benefit of stabilizing his breakfast hour, because his commitment to eating at home meant that everything he needed for breakfast was already in the house, and he could eat soon after rising. Richard began making himself breakfasts of oatmeal with nuts or whole-grain bread with healthy toppings, easy to eat at home, hard to eat on the go. His improved breakfast and more consistent meal hour gave him energy that carried him all the way through to lunch without a slump. Establishing a consistent breakfast routine also standardized Richard's lunch hour because he now became hungry at virtually the same hour of the afternoon every day. Once his mealtimes were clearly established, Richard ceased much of his between-meal snacking.

Whether you eat out or at home, eat oatmeal or eggs, you need to eat (and relish) a really good breakfast at a regular time to give your engine the best start to its long day. Your first resolution could be to eliminate or include certain foods at breakfast, to cease eating beyond a certain hour at night, or to establish a stable time and place for breakfast. Whatever you resolve, be absolutely relentless in establishing your new habit— nailing breakfast brings huge engine benefits.

Don't Treat Nutrition as a Zero-Sum Game

So often diets force us into desperate trade-offs between healthy foods and the sugary snacks we feel we need to quiet overwhelming cravings. *If I eat an apple*, we reason, *that's a hundred calories, but what I really, really want is a chocolate-chip cookie*. It's a false choice, because these foods are equivalent only in their calories, not in their nutritional value. But we lust for the cookie, so we skip the apple. We miss out on the apple's nutrients and the fiber that will keep us fuller longer. And we continue to crave the poor foods we associate with a boost in mood and energy, rather than developing a taste for the crisp freshness of an apple. One of my early diet microresolutions was to add two whole fruits to what I ate each day, rather than trying to substitute fruit for a favorite snack, such as chocolate. Eating more fruit killed some of my taste for sweets, and the extra fiber kept me from getting hungry before dinner. Now I often crave fruit, the same way I used to crave sugar. Do I still eat sweets? Yes, but less frequently and in smaller quantities.

Salad Days

Kathy generally ate in the office cafeteria, usually selecting a hot entrée that was rich in meat or cheese. She knew that her weight and nutrition would improve if she chose salad for lunch more often, but she enjoyed the hot lunch, and the salad didn't satisfy her. When Kathy began looking for a microresolution to enhance her daily nutrition, she decided to eat salad at lunch with her entrée. Adding the salad meant that she was getting an extra serving of leafy green vegetables every day, a real nutrition boost. Over time Kathy began to enjoy her salad as much as the entrée, and she was able to pump up the salad size and skinny down the richer portions of her meal. Sometimes she just had a big salad or a salad and a cup of soup. Her micro-resolution to *include* salad improved her diet and over time made it possible for her to be satisfied with a less rich lunch. The single resolution helped put Kathy on the road to *satisfied with less*.

Fruits and vegetables are essential to a healthy, self-regulating engine. They fill you up, stave off disease, and provide vitamins, minerals, and fiber. New research shows that adding pureed vegetables to dishes such as macaroni and cheese results in consuming significantly fewer calories and more nutrients, without loss of enjoyment.* If your diet is low in fruits and vegetables, consider a resolution to add these foods to what you already eat, rather than fretting about what you'll have to give up to "fund" these healthful additions. Adding more fruits and vegetables will improve your nutritional profile, increase your satisfaction, help reduce cravings for poorer foods, and ultimately change your tastes.

Hydration

Thirst is often mistaken for hunger, leading us to eat when it's really water our body craves. According to the University of Tennessee, 75 percent of Americans are in a state of chronic dehydration, and 37 percent experience such weak thirst

---

* Alexandra D. Blatt et al., "Hidden Vegetables: An Effective Strategy to Reduce Energy Intake and Increase Vegetable Intake in Adults," *American Journal of Clinical Nutrition* 93, no. 4 (April 2011): 756–63.

signaling that by the time they feel true thirst they are seriously dehydrated.* Water is essential to keeping your body and brain running at peak. Staying ahead of the hydration curve improves brain function, elevates mood, supports short-term memory, boosts endurance, protects against injury, enhances athletic performance, and aids in keeping you feeling full and satisfied.

Good hydration improves the performance of your engine. A 2003 study at the University of Utah showed that dehydration leads to a decline in metabolism of around 2 percent per day.† In a more recent study, middle-aged and older dieters who consumed sixteen ounces of water before each meal achieved a 44 percent greater weight loss than those who ate the same diet without drinking extra water.‡

Despite water's importance to overall health and weight loss, the eight-glass rule is usually marginalia in diet books, where the attention of both writer and reader is on what food is allowed on the plan. Building a water habit, as with all habits, requires dedicated focus. But once good hydration becomes your new normal, when your hydration level starts to slip you'll automatically begin to sip.

Within Reach

Theresa often went through the day drinking little or no water. Rather than setting herself a water quota, she made a micro-resolution *to keep a water bottle at work and refill it when empty*. This resolution targeted convenience and availability and did not include a mandate to drink more.

---

* University of Tennessee, Extension (Department of Agriculture), "Did You Know These Important Facts About Water?" June 2008.
† *Health and Healing* 13, no. 7 (July 2003).
‡ *Obesity* (Silver Spring) 18, no. 2(February 2010): 300–307.

Once water was always at hand, Theresa's water consumption began to rise. The first few days, she seldom drank all twenty ounces of water, but by the second week she was refilling the bottle by late afternoon. By the third week she generally drained the bottle twice during working hours. "I used to work at my desk and only get up for coffee when I began to feel tired. But because I now always have water right in front of me, I keep sipping it. Water is more than a habit for me now; it's almost an addiction."

One microresolution I made that increased my water consumption was simply *to drink one glass of water for every glass of wine*. My microresolution meant making sure that I had a glass of water at the table, and I often drank the entire glass of water as soon as I sat down, rather than reaching for wine to satisfy my thirst. Once I made my resolution, I often found myself drinking two or three glasses of water during the meal and I saw my wine consumption drop from two glasses to one glass, a savings of about 150 calories a day. Drinking water at dinnertime kept me from getting dehydrated during the evening, and I stopped waking up at night feeling thirsty or with the occasional light headache.

Appetite

I once had a terrible flu that lasted for several days, during which I couldn't eat a thing; I just sipped water, slept, and retched. When I finally felt a little better, I made myself some plain rice with a bit of salt. I was so hungry that the aroma from that humble bowl of rice intoxicated me and I felt close to drooling. My stomach had shrunk, so I ate very slowly. The rice tasted incredibly delicious and felt like a wave of pure energy entering my exhausted body. I can't remember a meal that gave me more pleasure or satisfaction.

We needn't starve ourselves in order appreciate the food we eat, but to be fully awake to the glories of eating, we at least need to exhaust what we consumed at our last meal before we eat again. When you arrive at the table already full from snacking, you cheat yourself out of the greatest pleasure in dining, and you'll likely leave the table feeling overfull and sluggish (and thinking about eating something sweet to shake off the lethargy that comes with overeating).

Microresolutions can help you reform your eating behaviors so that you're hungry at mealtime, experience greater eating satisfaction, and you burn nutrients more efficiently. If you regularly sit down to dinner or lunch with anything less than true hunger, examine your eating behaviors to pinpoint a change that will better align your hunger with mealtimes. It could be dropping a snack, retiming a snack, eating a lighter snack, or exercising before a meal to burn off some excess fuel. Making just one microresolution to reduce snacking or up your exercise can have a profound effect on your long-term weight and eating satisfaction.

Ready for Dinner

Robert generally didn't snack in the afternoon at work and looked forward to the congenial meal he shared with his family each evening. Robert's habit on arriving home was to get a cold beer from the refrigerator along with some salty pretzels to eat with it. The beer was filling in itself, and the addition of a couple of handfuls of pretzels often meant that by the time he sat down to dinner he had already consumed several hundred calories. Yet even without true appetite, he still ate a full meal with his family and often left the table feeling overfull.

In his quest to lose some weight, Robert reconsidered his predinner snack habit. He didn't want to give up his beer ritual—it relaxed him after a long day of work—so he focused instead on reducing the impact that the salty snack had on his waistline and his dinner appetite. The beer was typically 160 calories and the pretzels around 200. Robert made a microresolution *to limit predinner snacks to 50 calories*. He made a list of salty treats equaling 50 calories: five small pretzels, five chips, six olives, three medium pickles. The pretzels and chips, Robert quickly found, left him wanting more, but the pickle kept him off the addictive carbs while delivering a salty wallop. Missing the crunch of the pretzels, he began eating celery sticks along with the pickles and beer. In reforming a single snack habit, Robert better aligned his appetite to dinner and saved himself 150 calories a day, enough to lose fifteen pounds over three years, according to the latest weight-loss models.*

If you make a microresolution aimed at increasing your hunger for real meals, be sure you know what hunger feels like. In our culture of plenty, we often use the word "hunger" to describe any idle urge to eat, confusing *cravings* with *hunger*. Hunger is a growling stomach, a cry that the body has exhausted its fuel, not suddenly feeling in the mood for Chips Ahoy. You can be full of food—the opposite of hungry—and still crave something to eat, very often something sweet. Craving carbohydrates in the absence of hunger is an energy distress signal from a tired brain and body; one strategy to relieve such cravings is to treat these urges

---

* Kevin D. Hall et al., "Quantification of the Effect of Energy Imbalance on Bodyweight," *Lancet* 378, no. 9793 (August 27, 2011): 826–37.

chemically. Rather than letting the craving be a cue to toss back a handful of cookies or candy, make a microresolution *to respond to carbohydrate cravings with simple sugars*—a mint, a date, sweet tea or coffee. This will give your brain a direct sugar hit without the extra fat and calories that come with a carbohydrate-rich treat. One friend of mine who often indulged in afternoon confections made a microresolution *to swallow a teaspoon of honey when craving sweets*, a twenty-two-calorie hit of pure energy that saved her hundreds of calories each day. Making a no-excuses resolution requires that you be prepared when the craving hits, whether that's having a jar of honey or a box of Altoids in your desk drawer.

If you reform your habits to preserve your appetite for meals, your pleasure in dining will increase tremendously. Rather than minimizing the importance of food in an effort to eat less, maximize its importance by investing in wonderful meals consumed with a full appetite. Cultivating your appetite for meals will strengthen the association of eating with hunger, rather than with entertainment, boredom, or depression. Once you reform your eating so that you are sitting down to real meals with real appetite, you'll be on the path to better health, greater satisfaction, and weight loss.

Mindful Eating

Mindful eating is, first and foremost, enjoying every bit of what you eat. Every time you eat something without savoring it fully, stuff food into your mouth while driving, bolt down a meal between appointments, or dutifully finish every last bite of a soggy, tasteless sandwich, you're robbing yourself of enjoyment and satisfaction. The hundreds of calories you consume every day without awareness or full enjoyment are very likely the difference between your weight now and the weight you want to be. Microresolutions can help you eliminate mindless eating behaviors and increase your eating consciousness and enjoyment.

Food for Thought

Mindful eating means cultivating full sensory awareness of the foods you eat in order to achieve greater satisfaction and appreciation. So how's this for a microresolution? *I will only finish eating a food I am enjoying.* Recognize when what you're eating is giving you no real pleasure and *stop*. Mealy apples, overcooked meat, waxy cheese, gummy pasta, tasteless sandwiches, pressboard cookies, sour chocolate—don't dull your senses or waste your calories on unsatisfying food at home or when eating out. It's disappointing to order something in a restaurant, look forward to it, and then discover that it's totally *blah*, but there's no point in compounding dissatisfaction with a lackluster entrée by spending calories on it as well. Don't throw good calories after bad—stop eating the disappointment and eat something you can enjoy instead.

As most of your eating is done on autopilot, you're programmed to finish what you're eating even when it isn't giving you any real pleasure. You have to practice asking yourself, *Am I really enjoying this?** I save myself calories every day and up my

---

* A caveat here: If you're trying to add more fruits, vegetables, and whole grains to your diet and at first you don't find these foods enjoyable to eat, you need to keep them in your diet long enough to develop a taste for them. These nutrients are so important to your health that you can't drop them from your diet even if you don't enjoy them. However, once you learn to love them, you can apply the same "*must enjoy*" rule: no point in eating a healthy piece of whole-grain toast that tastes like sawdust.

satisfaction levels by practicing this simple habit. If it isn't delicious, I just stop eating. Who said dieting isn't fun?

Make a Meal of It

Truman Capote famously said of Jack Kerouac that he didn't *write*, he *typed*, and most of us don't *dine*, we *eat*.

In rule 4 ("A microresolution is personal") I recounted at length my resolution *to savor my food and drink*. My resolution was meant to reform my habit of eating so quickly that satiation signals from my brain registered only after I had unwittingly blown straight past satisfaction to lead balloon. Eating more slowly by savoring every bite did indeed often lead me to lay down my fork before my plate was empty. My resolution was focused on enjoyment, not denial, and was far more effective in reducing my food consumption than any of my previous self-admonitions to eat less. As I learned to experience the pleasure of relaxing at meals, I began to invest more in the food, atmosphere, setting, and conversation. I learned how to dine instead of eat.

Studies show that children of families who share a dinner hour perform better in school and on standardized tests, are more successful, have higher self-esteem and more positive peer relationships, and are less likely to become overweight or involved with drugs.* The findings apply to two-parent as well as single-parent households, both affluent and poor. The conclusions in this research didn't surprise me at all—dining with friends or family provides a haven of well-being in a busy,

---

* For a review of research on the benefits of family meals, see Purdue University Center for Families, Promoting Family Meals Project, "Family Meals Spell S-U-C-C-E-S-S," www.cfs.purdue.edu/cff/documents/promoting_meals/spellsuc cessfactsheet.pdf.

stressful day, where every person present is nourished by the warmth of the table, shared food and conversation, eating to satisfaction, and belonging. Eating is necessary to life; dining is essential to appreciation and community. If eating severally has become a habit in your family due to complex schedules that include working late, soccer practice, exercise class, or long commutes, consider making a microresolution that pulls the family together at least one more night a week, even if it means dining a bit later or giving up some discretionary activities.

Making microresolutions that put the focus on the ritual of dining and savoring every morsel of a meal can help you to lose weight by wringing pleasure out of every calorie. Food is something to be celebrated, to be grateful for, to relish. The more you truly appreciate and enjoy your food—the more you *value* it—the more likely you are to find yourself satisfied with less of it.

Drive-Through Eating

Our 24/7 eating habits are driven by mindless responses to environmental cues. If you'd like to lose weight, taking notice of the times you habitually eat with less-than-full awareness or enjoyment will expose fat targets for microresolutions.

Do you ever eat in line, snack from the grocery cart, or eat your breakfast doughnut in the elevator on the way up to your office? Have you ever bought a hot dog at a sporting event and finished eating it before you made it back to your seat? Do you circle free-sample food tables so that you can get more than one taste? Do you eat while you prepare food and scarf up the leftovers of others?

I was once standing behind someone in a cafeteria line who was eating off her tray as she waited to pay. Before she reached the front of the line, she had eaten most of the good stuff. How much pleasure could she have derived from such a meal? Not too much, because when she found herself next in line to pay, she broke out of the line and went back to get dessert! I would have laughed if I hadn't identified with her entirely. A simple microresolution not to eat until seated might have turned the unsatisfied grazer into a happy diner.

Eating while walking, driving, or commuting is another way to gain weight mindlessly and rob food of its full pleasure. If you are an on-the-go type who can eat a taco while crossing the street or lo mein with chopsticks while shifting gears, ask yourself how much more you might enjoy these "meals" if you actually sat still to eat them, and make yourself a microresolution that results in greater awareness and appreciation of mealtime. Dude, *sit down*.

Yet sitting itself doesn't guarantee conscious eating. Eating in front of the TV or the computer, while talking on the phone or texting, or even during a meeting at work dulls your appreciation and makes it harder to achieve real satisfaction. A meal consumed on autopilot will likely leave you yearning for "something else" when it concludes.

Breaking Bread

Jerry nearly always ate lunch at work in front of his computer, fielding phone calls and e-mails for the bare ten minutes it took him to consume his sandwich. Worse, if he was called into a meeting and had just sat down to lunch, he would wolf down his sandwich and wash it down with a drink in two minutes flat. Jerry craved sugar almost immediately after eating his shot-clock lunch and usually snacked heavily in the afternoon. He wondered if he could reduce or eliminate his snack cravings if he made more of a meal out of lunch. Jerry made a microresolu-tion *to eat lunch away from my desk.*

The first week of his resolution, he ate at a table in his office away from the phone and computer but found it more anxiety provoking than relaxing. Hearing the phone ring and seeing the meaningful glances his assistant passed him through the glass door drove him back to his desk at least once during his short lunch. So Jerry began eating in the cafeteria, something he hadn't done regularly since he graduated from cube to office. Eating away from his office reduced interruptions to the urgent, and Jerry began taking more time to eat and relax. To make his meal last a full half hour, he made a second microresolution: to always begin his cafeteria lunches with a cup of soup. Eating the hot soup helped him relax into the meal and take his time, rather than treating lunch as a quick refueling pit stop. And while Jerry hadn't been seeking company when he began eating in the caf-eteria, he found plenty of it. He ended up visiting and exchang-ing ideas with colleagues whom he wouldn't otherwise have seen during the workday. Sometimes he joined a group of trainees from his team for lunch, giving him a chance to get unfiltered feedback on what the best, brightest, and newest people thought worked (or didn't) in his department. Jerry's lunch in the cafete-ria became an important part of his day, establishing a break from task-driven work and encouraging networking and closer contact with his team. Taking longer to eat lunch (thirty minutes instead of five) did indeed increase his satisfaction and make it possible for him to resist treats in the late afternoon more often. Jerry gained greater satisfaction, ate less, lost weight, increased his work network, and became a better manager, all from mak-ing two microresolutions.

It's a battle to eat consciously in our multitasking, fast-food culture. More and more companies cater to our penchant for eating on the go. I recently read an article in *USA Today** about a scary new restaurant offering called Cup O'Pancakes designed to fit into the cup holder of a car so that you can eat pancakes while driving, no fork necessary! Can Feedbag O'Pancakes be far behind? Yet another new fast-food item is "popcorn chicken," a snack/meal that allows you to toss back greasy meat pellets as you drive or walk, the same way you toss back popcorn in a movie theater. Make no mistake: There's plenty of money to be made by encouraging people to eat less and less consciously more and more often. Practicing resolutions that increase mindful eating can help keep you from filling every empty spot in the day with fast food and snacks.

Food should be a headliner, not a sideshow. Consider microresolutions that increase your consciousness and pleasure in dining, and eating less will follow. A microresolution *to start lunch on weekdays with a cup of hot soup* could stretch your meal, increase your satisfaction, and redirect attention to your food, simply because hot soup means eating more carefully. Similarly, making a resolution *to begin a meal by eating six doll-size bites* will establish a slower, more conscious rhythm for your meal and stop you from inhaling your plate as soon as it's in front of you. Resolutions that get you to savor and slow down will pay huge dividends. Pay attention! Enjoy more! Eat less!

Less

Practicing mindful eating and cultivating habits that keep your metabolism fired up will make it easier for you to achieve

---

* "Marketers Adapt Menus to Eat-When-I-WantTrend," *USA Today*, November 22, 2011.

satisfaction while eating less, but to lose weight you will have to eat fewer calories than you eat today, period. Using microresolutions, you can achieve permanent weight loss by targeting specific behavioral changes that reduce the number of calories you consume each day.

In the introduction to this book, I talked about my microresolution to stop eating catered cookies in conference rooms at work. I succeeded in my resolution, but after several months of abstaining, my weight had dipped only slightly. "Can you believe," I said to my hairdresser (with whom I discuss all such topics), "that I eliminated all those calories and didn't lose more weight?" "Hey, that's the ten pounds you would have *gained*," he said (proving himself indeed to be the fount of wisdom I had always taken him for). My *no conference room cookies* pledge helped me to shed a couple of pounds but, more critically, halted the upward trajectory of my weight. We diet veterans often think that when we're not actively dieting, we're maintaining, when in fact we're slowly gaining.

My friend Vivian, who worked hard to stay trim all her adult life, gave herself a pass during pregnancy and indulged in all the treats she had fought against eating for so many years. She expected the weight she gained to disappear after giving birth, but months later she was still fifteen pounds heavier than she had been before her pregnancy. Instead of jumping on the diet bandwagon, Vivian decided to embrace what she called her "Rubenesque" self and continue to enjoy the treats that had comforted her during her pregnancy. She believed she had made a smart and mature decision not to try to reduce to her prebaby weight.

But rather than staying at the weight she had accepted as her new normal, Vivian blew right past it into new territory.

Within a year she had put on five pounds more, and a year further on, another three. Vivian didn't add more calories; she simply continued to eat the daily treats she had eaten in pregnancy. Since the extra calories were marginally more than what she needed to maintain her weight, she continued to gain slowly.

These examples demonstrate how the battle to maintain a healthy weight is fought *at the margin*. Adding one new snack or a second beer or eating only slightly richer meals will see you creeping up the scale. A 2011 study published in the *Lancet* by Dr. Kevin D. Hall and colleagues at the National Institutes of Health put forward a new and more finely calibrated model of how caloric increases and decreases affect people of different weight and body composition over time.* Dr. Hall's studies show that eating just ten extra calories a day will raise the weight of an average person by twenty pounds over thirty years, so imagine what an extra cookie a day can do. But the battle to lose weight permanently is also *won* at the margin. Dr. Hall's model shows that for every pound of weight you want to lose, cutting ten calories permanently from your daily diet will result in losing half the weight the first year and almost 95 percent of the weight after three years.† If your goal is to lose twenty pounds, eliminating two hundred calories from your diet will find you ten pounds slimmer by the end of the first year and virtually at your goal in three (to achieve a loss of twenty pounds in a single year, you'd have to cut out four hundred calories). It's likely that many of the calories you'd need to shed are consumed mindlessly at the margin of real meals and healthful snacks. All

---

* Hall et al., "Quantification of the Effect of Energy Imbalance on Bodyweight."
† The slowing of weight loss over this time period is due to changes in body composition and energy expenditure as weight is lost.

you need to do to achieve permanent weight loss is to lock in a marginal behavior change that shaves off some of these calories. So ask yourself: What's at the margin?

When You Eat

One way to drop calories from your diet is to examine the times of day and occasions when you eat outside of mealtime and target one for elimination through a microresolution. It could be a midmorning snack (weak breakfast), afternoon snack (afternoon slump), Frappuccino for the ride home (reward after work), or late-night snack (stimulant). If you don't think you can entirely eliminate a snack in your schedule, look to reduce its caloric impact, either by eating half of what you've become accustomed to or by eating something lighter in its place.

Sometimes you don't need to eliminate a snack but just change its timing, its *when*. If you habitually binge on simple carbs at 5:00 p.m. when you're a couple of hours from dinner but too hungry to wait, you may be able to save calories, avoid hunger, and cultivate more appetite for dinner by making a microresolution to snack earlier in the day. A microresolution *to eat a snack I have prepared every day at 3:00 p.m.* will give you a lift, stave off hunger, and still allow you to arrive at dinner with good appetite. Including the language of "preparation" in your microresolution will ensure that your snack is planned, not ad hoc. Casting about for a snack spells doom, while planning a snack puts you in control and forces you to think through and prepare a snack that is healthy, satisfying, and right-sized. In order to stick to a time and be ready with a decent snack, you'll need to go at your resolution with rigor, because preparing a snack to bring to work each day (even one you buy on the way in) won't happen if you give it only casual attention.

Another way to cut calories outside of mealtime is to set your sights on disrupting opportunistic snacking cues. For example, making a microresolution *not to eat while preparing food* will keep you from eating an extra slice of cheese while making a sandwich; a microresolution *to eat only from my own plate* will keep you from finishing the hot cocoa you made your kid. A resolution only *to eat food in a bar that I order for myself* will keep you from autopiloting over to happy-hour plates of potato skins and fried mozzarella. Circumventing just one of these cues permanently will make a long-term difference in your weight.

BYO

Keith often partook of treats made available on the desks of office coworkers. The bull pen with a fishbowl full of minis at its center, the jar of chocolate-covered mints at reception, the macadamia-nut clusters brought into the office by an employee just returned from Hawaii, tins of candied popcorn sent to the office by a vendor for the holidays. He not only took these treats when casually encountered but also found himself searching out such offerings as the day wore on, his self-control weakening as he grew more tired.

In order to combat his foraging, Keith made a microresolution to eat only treats at the office that he himself provided. Now if he wanted an afternoon snack, he would have to plan for it rather than snacking mindlessly. Replacing his untracked, opportunistic office noshing with a planned snack forced Keith to account fully for what he ate each day and drop calories from his daily diet.

Another *when* worth a microresolution may be how long you give yourself before giving in to a craving for something less than healthy. Many of us experience a keen desire for something sweet when we finish a meal and digestion begins to slow our metabolism, and it's at that moment we are most vulnerable to eating our way past comfortable fullness into food-coma territory. But if you make a microresolution *to wait fifteen minutes after a meal before eating anything else*, you may find that the craving for something sweet subsides on its own. Waiting is hard, but once you've trained yourself to do it, you'll find that you pretty much forget to check in after fifteen minutes. And whenever I want to overeat a tasty something, I send myself this message: *Overstuffed is a miserable feeling.*

What You Eat

You can use microresolutions to save calories at the margin and lose weight by making discrete changes to the mix of foods you regularly eat. Any time you substitute a healthier food for a less healthy food, it's a win for your engine, and any time you swap out a high-calorie food for a lower-calorie food, it's a win for your waistline. Such swaps lock in calorie savings that lead to permanent weight loss while maintaining overall diet satisfaction.

One simple microresolution food swap I made was to use skim milk in place of whole milk in coffee. I used to make this substitution only when whooping down the diet warpath, and as soon my willpower folded I would return to my previous eating habits and richer brews. But when I began making permanent, marginal behavioral changes through microresolutions, I resolved *to use only skim milk in coffee and tea.* At that time I was drinking, on average, three cups of decaf coffee a day, each with half a cup or more of whole milk, for a total of 240 calories. The simple substitution of skim milk saved me 135 calories a day, and I didn't even think of it as dieting, just a behavioral change it made sense to make *forever*. Every such saving you lock in will contribute to permanent weight loss. Now I prefer skim milk, I don't feel cheated or deprived, and the calorie savings are locked in, my new normal.

If you regularly experience a midafternoon slump and you can't nap it off, a microresolution *to limit afternoon carbs to tea and honey* (or coffee and sugar) will give you the boost you crave without packing on the extra fat and calories that come with a richer snack. The sweetened tea lifts your energy with 50 calories, the candy bar with 220. The hot tea will take longer to consume and give your brain a chance to register new energy and signal satisfaction. If you presently give in to a rich treat most afternoons, making this single microresolution could be the difference between your weight now and the weight you'd like to be.

If meat is the centerpiece of your evening meal, resolving *to eat fish two nights a week for dinner* will save you hundreds of calories as well as boost your health and create variety in your diet. If your diet is rich in fried foods, resolving *to eat fried food no more than once a week* would improve your health (even to the point of increasing your life span), likely result in weight loss, and sensitize your palate to lighter fare and subtler flavors. My guess is that adopting either one of these resolutions would ultimately increase dining pleasure as well as lead to better health and weight outcomes.

Making microresolutions that substitute whole foods for refined foods advances both weight loss and nutrition. Generally, the more refined a food, the more concentrated its sugars and calories: orange juice versus an orange; Cheerios versus oatmeal; potato chips versus a baked potato. Sugar and flour are the most highly refined culprits in the modern diet. While dieters know to avoid sugar, flour generally accounts for more empty calories in a day of eating. If you eat two pieces of toast at breakfast, two pieces of sandwich bread at lunch, and a couple of pieces of bread at dinner, that's around six hundred calories a day just on bread, and if it's all white bread that's six hundred *empty* calories. And that's just bread; pasta, pizza, packaged cereals, pretzels, chips, crackers, cookies, cake—even Twizzlers—are made with flour. When you add it all up, a huge portion of what should be healthy baseline calories is occupied by refined flour, which almost instantly turns into sugar in the digestive system. The sugar provides a rush but burns out quickly, leaving you prone to heavy snacking before your next meal.

Making resolutions that eliminate some white-flour items from your eating will improve your nutrition, help you lose weight, and begin to wean you from a sugar-based diet. Linda's resolution to give up flour-based foods at lunch (recounted in chapter 9) is a great open-frame resolution. Ending her reliance on refined flour as a lunch mainstay led her to eat a healthier variety of foods and to slim down.

I made a series of microresolutions aimed at reducing the caloric impact of flour in my diet. My first resolution was *to eat whole grains for breakfast on weekdays.* That meant no toast, muffins, bagels, or refined cereals. In place of these bakery items, I began by eating a high-fiber muesli cereal and ended by falling in love with oatmeal, so much so that I have it even on those weekend days not covered by my resolution. Getting flour out of breakfast changed my eating and energy patterns for the whole day. First of all, hot oatmeal makes a real bowlful that takes time to eat and is immensely satisfying. Adding fresh fruit, nuts, and nut milk to the mix makes the oatmeal even more delicious and nutritious. The oatmeal, nuts, and fruit are so high in fiber that I don't get hungry for at least five hours, and my energy burns steadily the entire morning without any slumps. By lunchtime I have a big appetite for something as real, delicious, and wholesome as my breakfast. It wasn't until I made my *whole grain* resolution that I realized that eating sugar for breakfast corrupts the whole day's energy and eating pattern.

My next microresolution target was dinner bread. I grew up with French bread at dinner and continued that practice at my own table, but in examining my diet for the next eating shift to make at the margin, dinner bread stood out as a fat target. Two pieces are close to two hundred calories (even without butter) and add nothing nutritionally, so I resolved *to eat nothing from the breadbasket at dinner*. When I really have a hankering for French bread, I have it as a treat, because that's what it is. I sit down with my bread and maybe some butter and give it my full attention, relishing every bite of this savory dessert, but it's no longer a habitual part of my evening meal.

Eliminating so much sugar from my diet helped to stabilize my appetite and cravings throughout the day and kept me on the path to my ideal weight. I didn't rid my diet entirely of flour (can't live without pasta), but limiting it resulted in my eating larger portions of healthier, more fibrous, and less caloric foods. Experiencing the engine and weight-loss benefits of banishing flour-based breakfasts and French bread from dinner changed my mindset, and I began avoiding flour at lunch (sandwiches, pizza) and for snacks (cookies, pretzels, corn chips). Flour is so pervasive in the modern diet that limiting it is a boon to the eating imagination. I eat far more fruits, vegetables, nuts, salads, and soups now that I don't reach for flour every time I'm hungry.

Capitalizing on opportunities to swap out high-calorie items in your habitual diet for lower-calorie, healthier foods could save you the calories you need to reach your weight goal. These substitutions can lead to weight loss, better nutrition, and a more varied and satisfying diet. Your choices will be based on how you eat now. Start with the man in the mirror and look for modifications you can make permanent through a change in habit.

How Much

As a young teenager I once went camping with a friend's family in Lake Tahoe. One evening we left the shore of the lake to go to a casino, where the adults did a bit of gambling and the kids a bit of gamboling. The highlight was a visit to an all-you-can-eat buffet. All around me people piled their plates high with mismatched entrees such as beef, pork, fish, and pasta; mashed *and* baked potatoes. My girlfriend and I spent most of our time hauling different desserts back to our booth—cakes, pies, cookies, and puddings. The food was really terrible—not even the desserts were good—but all around us people were going back for more, as if trying to make back at the buffet what they had lost at the gaming tables. But large portions are a losing bet at the dining table, where practicing portion control is essential for winning at the weight-loss game.

Portion sizes in our society have never been bigger, and it's sad that in our culture we often confuse *size* with *value*. Rather than finding satisfaction in healthy and delicious foods, we seek satisfaction in *more* food. And since we're a society of fast eaters (not leisurely diners), we serve ourselves giant portions just to make our meal last longer than fifteen minutes.

Many diets are based entirely on portion control. On these programs, strict portion sizes are prescribed across all meals and snacks, and those who can sustain the smaller portion sizes forever will lose weight and keep it off. For others the drastic and comprehensive reduction proves overwhelming, and when they quit dieting they revert to the portion sizes they favored previously. But you needn't start by cutting the portions of everything you eat. Instead, target a reduction in a single food portion until eating less of it is routine. By identifying an item you habitually eat and reducing its portion size, you can lock in calorie savings for a lifetime.

For example, I used to have a weekly appointment near a bakery that offered a delicious oatmeal and blueberry muffin. I knew this muffin had around five hundred calories, but I found it irresistible and looked forward to my appointment and the muffin every week. Recognizing that the extra calories were a threat to maintaining my weight, I made a microresolution to eat only half of the muffin. As soon as the muffin was in my hands, I broke off the top (the best part) and threw the rest away immediately. I can honestly say that I continued to enjoy my treat with just as much satisfaction as before. How is that possible when the snack was half as large? Well, because autopilot generally just finishes a food for us, even if we're already full and not really deriving any serious pleasure from continuing to eat. That's the genius behind those hundred-calorie cookie packs—you can finish the entire bag on autopilot rather than exerting the self-control required to eat just two Oreos in a six-cookie pack (*good luck with that*).

The empty treat bag may signal the end of snack time, but at mealtime many of us don't feel finished until we see an empty plate. *Clean your plate,* many of us learned as children. And it's when you face the empty plate that the urge for a second portion is triggered. Making a microresolution *to leave something on my plate at every meal* will short-circuit this powerful cue and help you realize that a meal is finished when you are satisfied, not when your plate shines. If you have to serve yourself a bit more in order to leave something uneaten, go ahead, because disrupting autopilot's finish fetish is powerfully important.

Coneheads

During the summer months, Will habitually went to an ice cream parlor with his family after dinner. The outing was a treat they all looked forward to, including taking a walk around the neighborhood in the warm summer night as they licked their cones. Wanting to trim calories yet participate in the family outing, Will made a microresolution to toss his cone after eating half the ice cream above the cone level, around a quarter cup. He licked the ice cream slowly and savored it to make it last. Will found that most of the pleasure in the cold creaminess was in the first several licks, not the last bite. He continued to look forward to the ice cream outing and didn't feel deprived, although the size of his treat had shrunk. "The hard part was just throwing the cone away when I was at my limit, but once I threw it away, I didn't miss it. I didn't walk the rest of the way wishing for more. Once I had tossed it, I felt as if I had finished it. Gone is gone."

Good-bye, Mr. Chips

Peter, a screenwriter, ate nearly the same lunch every day: a sandwich and a small bag of chips. The sandwich filling varied, but the general contours of the lunch were the same. He resolved to drop the bag of chips from his lunch routine, the single change he made to his eating habits, and lost eight pounds in four months. All Peter needs to do to lock in his weight loss is make the "no chips at lunch" rule permanent and change nothing else about his diet. Does this mean Peter will never eat chips again? No, it just means that chips will be an occasional treat, rather than a lunch mainstay.

There are many opportunities in any diet to make significant savings at the margin through portion control. A microresolution to *never eat more than three French fries at a time* will allow you to indulge but keep you out of trouble. If you currently eat a couple of cups of pasta a couple of times a week and you resolve *to enjoy a single cup of pasta at mealtimes,* you'll save yourself a load of calories. A cup of pasta will still be very satisfying and filling, especially if you prolong the pleasure by twirling the pasta around your fork a couple of strands at a time, rather than spooling a mouthful three inches in diameter. If you regularly eat eight ounces or more of meat at dinner, making a resolution *to limit meat portions to six ounces* may win the waistline battle for you and leave you more appetite for the delicious vegetables that are a requirement for good health and a happy engine. If you eat a sandwich every day for lunch, a microresolution *to eat only open-faced sandwiches on weekdays* will save you eighty to a hundred calories a day, just from removing the top slice of bread. To go further, make a microresolution *to eat no more than half a sandwich for weekday lunch,* and instead add an apple or some salad or soup. If you drink two beers every night, making a microresolution *to drink just one beer a day Monday through Thursday* will save you six hundred–plus calories a week while allowing you more leeway on the weekend. If you eat a whole bagel with cream cheese in the morning, eating three-quarters of it will save you at least a hundred calories a day. Each marginal reduction will move you down the scale in the same way small changes to your diet inched you up.

Where

Settings affect our dining experience and can in themselves cue us to overindulge. Visiting one's childhood home and smelling Mom's cooking can cue a teenage-sized appetite in an adult with a middle-aged metabolism. Sports arenas (and watching sports at home) can cue the desire for hot dogs, chips, fries, and lots of beer. Bars often offer greasy and salty happy-hour finger foods designed to induce the desire for another drink. Neighborhoods are full of eating cues—coffee houses, bakeries, pizzerias.

Examining the effect of place on your eating behavior can lead to good ideas for microresolutions. What you eat during half an hour of happy hour could be the caloric equivalent of a fourth meal. If you always go out for a drink with the gang on Friday nights, enjoy the greasy bar food, but then go home and eat dinner, your resolution could be *to choose between bar food and dinner on nights out with the gang,* which could cut five hundred calories from your weekly intake. Making a microresolution *to eat just half of everything served at Mom's* can save your Sunday visit from becoming a weekly setback. Where you physically sit to eat your meal may also affect your efforts to eat less. Eating dinner in front of the television, having lunch at the computer, or snacking while Skyping with a friend will limit your satisfaction and lead to the urge for more.

There's a famous deli my family loves in Brooklyn called Junior's, where we often eat before going to a show at the Brooklyn Academy of Music (BAM). After years of trying to order something low-cal in a high-cal place, I changed strategies and now order any deli sandwich I like and eat half of it. The Reuben sandwich I lust for is so huge that half of it is more than enough, and I usually don't finish it. I look forward to it, relish every single bite, and feel really full when I've finished. This resolution began as place specific, or least deli specific, but on its own it's turned into a flexible guideline that works whenever I'm in a situation where all the choices are pretty rich—I just eat part of what I'm served (very slowly).

When I was in my twenties, I told my doctor that although

I was eating "hardly anything," I wasn't losing weight. My doctor replied, "When someone tells me that they can't lose weight on an apple a day I say: 'Eat *half* an apple.'" Clearly the good doctor was skeptical about my claim that I ate *hardly anything*, but thinking about this exchange today, I realize his broader point is the critical one. However much you are eating now, if you change one behavior that results in eating less, you'll lose weight. It's all happening at the margin.

CHAPTER 13

Clutter

Resolution #2: Always put last night's panties in the
laundry basket.

—*Bridget Jones's Diary* (film)

"**N**eatness is the virtue of ordinary minds," goes the saying,
coined, perhaps, by smart, foxy people who believe
that extraordinary minds need not bother to develop
any conventional virtues. Scoffing at the ordinary isn't a good
idea, I've found, as even virtues you consider modest can prove
hard to acquire once you realize you're missing them. You may
discover all too late that *neatness counts*.

Neatness is so much a product of autopilot that its quiet efficiency can surprise. I had to work consciously to establish a
habit of hanging up kitchen towels neatly after a lifetime of
sinks decorated with damp wads; now when I go to straighten
up the dish-towel rack, I often find it has already been neatened
by the stealthy hand of autopilot. Hanging up my coat is by now
so ingrained that I end up hanging up other people's coats; I'm
just programmed to hang up coats whenever I see them draped
over chairs. Neatness habits work themselves so deeply into

autopilot that you can follow through with your routines in a nearly unconscious state.

Neatness standards are established early in family life, and most of us have additional neatness habits impressed on us by those we live with later on. The college roommate protests about a stack of newspapers on the floor, a love interest objects to a tube of toothpaste squeezed in the middle, an office mate complains about coffee cups serving as virtual petri dishes for unmanned experiments. Before I met my husband, I sometimes left dishes in the sink for hours after dinner (and sometimes until the next morning); he insisted that we clean up immediately, and now I can't conceive of doing it any other way. My siblings are much more relaxed about kitchen cleanup, which doesn't surprise me, because they grew up the same way I did and didn't marry my husband.

One often finds households where the public areas are neat and the private ones less so, reflecting a contract between co-habitants on standards for shared spaces. Sometimes there's a standoff, as in the play (and later TV show) *The Odd Couple*, where an obsessive-compulsive neatnik (Felix) and an utter slob (Oscar) take up residence together after suffering divorces. The friction makes for good comedy, mostly because no one in the audience would want to live with either one of them. If you think of Felix and Oscar as existing on opposite ends of a neatness scale with pathological neatness at one end and debilitating chaos at the other, you can see that one might select a neatness target at any point along the scale; the standard is personal. Whatever degree on this scale constitutes *neat* for you, the best way to achieve it is to move up one degree at a time by persistently practicing a new neatness habit or attitude until it sticks for good.

Just as your parent used endless repetition to teach you to wipe your feet on the doormat before entering the house (perhaps making you go back outside if you forgot), relentlessly practicing a microresolution of your own design can teach you a new neatness trick. If you're a total slob, your first microresolution might be as modest as keeping drawers and closet doors closed; further up the scale you might make a resolution *to prepare and dispose of recycling on Tuesday and Friday*, rather than letting it pile up until it overflows. You just keep picking off the next neatness pain point until you're reasonably happy with the tidiness that your autopilot now maintains for you.

A place for everything and everything in its place, goes another neatness adage, and you may find that when you test-drive your first neatness resolution, a place for something is lacking, hampering your follow-through. For example, if you resolve to keep your desk free of papers but you don't have a reasonable filing system, you'll need to create at least a minimal one; if you resolve to keep clothes from collecting on the bedroom chair but every bureau drawer is overstuffed, you'll need to either clear out items or find more drawer space. When I made my *just as fast to hang it up* resolution, I found that there weren't any free hangers in the closet and had to buy some. Neatness resolutions often require some reorganization of the home or workplace in order to get them on the road to autopilot. One of the many advantages of microresolutions is that their highly targeted nature sets in high relief the small changes required to grease the wheels of your resolution. For my *hang it up* resolution, I just had to remove some closet items and buy some hangers to make it work; I didn't have to clean out the whole closet.

One foe of *a place for everything* is too much stuff, a modern problem. The reality TV series *Hoarders* is devoted to profiling people whose lives are in danger because they can't throw anything away. Check out this episode description from the Web site of the series broadcaster, A&E:

> A victim of abuse as a child, Diana's hoarding became so extreme that her daughter was forced to sleep in a recliner because the trash had overtaken her room. But now a neighbor has blown the whistle on the heap, and the house could be condemned if Diana doesn't clean up fast. Meanwhile, Dolores was once an antiques dealer with such a great eye for value that she even sold to Sotheby's. But her buying got out of hand, and now she's got a hoard that could catch on fire and burn her house down at any time.

And you thought you were a slob! Every couple of years in New York someone is found dead among piles of newspapers dating back to 1900 and closets full of tchotchkes that weren't ever unboxed because there wasn't any shelf space left to display them, yet they all end up as an exhibit on the cover of the *New York Post*. If you have too much of something, you need to toss or store enough of it (see chapter 18, "Organization") in order to free adequate space to enable order.

But if it's just everyday clutter that's your problem, a neatness resolution to help segregate untidiness may be a useful starting point. Resolutions that enforce an area's particular utility—papers on desks, coins and jewelry on bureau, mail on the hall table—help create a crude order that can be refined over time as more neatness habits take hold.

Design for Living

Brian and Dorrie were both neatness challenged, their marriage one of not complementary but kindred habits. Each had a study in the home stacked with papers and books that they took back and forth to work. But items from the studies could also be found on the kitchen table, on the dining room table, and in the living room, which also played host to a child, a dog, and visitors. Work papers and books regularly collected on the coffee table, on bookshelves, and in piles by the couch that might also contain newspapers, magazines, and coloring books. Briefcases were sometimes splayed open on the floor, and crayons and pencils posed a hazard to those who dropped distractedly onto the couch. Hosting any social event at home meant a major cleanup, and drop-in visitors provoked scrambling and apologies.

Brian and Dorrie's first neatness microresolution was a joint one, aimed strictly at containment: *zero tolerance for briefcases, books, and papers left in the living room.* It was okay to read and study in the living room, but as soon as work was finished or interrupted, the books and papers had to be put back into the studies. This rule was strictly enforced even if the interruption was dinner, and work was to resume afterward.

Although they had for many years resolved at the New Year to become tidier, this microresolution was the first neatness pledge Brian and Dorrie ever managed to keep. The resolution was a simple one, as there were studies nearby to stash the books, papers, and briefcases that had collected, but for the first few weeks there was a collective groan every time they had to pack up before going out or sitting down to dinner. But after weeks of repetition, a new normal took hold in the living room, which became the one oasis of order in their chaotic household. It was pleasurable to sit down in the tidy living room, conducive to relaxing and conversing as well as studying. In "Magic Rose Geranium" style, Brian and Dorrie eventually extended their microresolution to include the dining room table and their child, whom they taught to pack up her papers and art projects and take them to her bedroom as soon as she had finished.

While the bedrooms and studies remained disorderly, the public spaces were always presentable. Having a mess-free zone for family life created greater relaxation and appetite for increased order, and new microresolutions followed. Best of all, Brian and Dorrie didn't have to think twice about extending invitations to friends or neighbors to come over and visit.

No Mess Is an Island

When Rebecca and her family moved away from Manhattan to a house in the suburbs, her new kitchen included a kitchen island. Immediately, the island became the drop-off point for whatever anyone brought into the house—groceries, mail, backpacks, umbrellas, hats, garden tools. Since the front door opened into the kitchen, the island became the logical place to unload, but it also created an overall impression of clutter. Once the island filled up, it became difficult to work in the kitchen without first conducting a cleanup, a problem in the morning when time was at a premium.

Rebecca resolved *never to leave a nonkitchen item on the island*. Keeping the kitchen island clear created more order in the central hub of the house and kept the work surface clear for cooking or eating while sitting on one of the island's bar stools. Rebecca created new storage to house the items that used to take up residence on the island—a coatrack for hats and gloves, a drawer dedicated to mail, a bin for any item that needed to be put away elsewhere (such as toys and tools). Opening the front door and seeing a clutter-free space helped motivate Rebecca to keep her house neat and clutter free.

Desk Set

Alan was an accomplished writer and lawyer whose workweek included book writing, legal work, teaching, blogging for a celebrated magazine, and speech writing. All this varied work converged on his desk at home, which on any given day might be cluttered with papers, mail, coffee cups, books, and research materials. During periods of stress the desk piles would grow out of control, and Alan felt his productivity was hampered by his disorderly environment. At the end of each day he told himself he should clean up, but he was often too tired or pressed by evening commitments to follow through.

Alan made a microresolution *to clean up my desk as the first task in my working day*. No sitting down to work until the desk was completely orderly. Each morning he would remove food wrappers and coffee cups, stack and sort mail, toss drafts, and file any papers he needed to keep for reference. Only when his desk was clear did Alan begin to work. As he was eager to get to work each morning, he brought tremendous energy and motivation to the performance of his new behavior. Sitting down to an orderly work space each day improved his neatness mindset, and he found himself tidying his desk more during the day than before he had made his morning cleanup resolution. Finally, the daily clearing of the desk forced more everyday organization— better files, up-to-date to-do lists, and desk organizers. Small move, big change.

No Vacancy

Sam regularly did the laundry but hated putting the laundry away. The laundry bag would sit on the floor for days, and he would just grab the items he needed directly from the bag, only managing to fully unload it days later. The bag's semipermanent occupancy on the floor seemed to attract other items, such as bags of toiletries bought at the drugstore or a box of paper for the printer, until there was a little pile. Sam made a microresolution *to bring the laundry bag into the bedroom only when I am ready to unpack it*. Once he began working his microresolution without excuses, he realized his procrastination in unloading the laundry was due to insufficient drawer space, so unloading was never fast and always frustrating. Sam bought a tall and narrow chest of drawers just for socks, underwear, and T-shirts. This made unpacking the laundry a breeze. To this first neatness resolution Sam added a resolution to remove all purchases from bags right away. Making the individual items visible turned out to be the key to getting them put away more quickly.

It's amazing how a space that is kept neater in just a single respect creates both greater calm and energy: in the bedroom, the bed; in the bathroom, towels; in the kitchen, dishes; in the foyer, mail; in the office, the desk; in the living room, the coffee table. A single new neatness habit can make a tremendous difference in the quality of your living and lead to less stress, more productivity, increased contentment, and a taste for greater order.

My friend Maria once said to me, "Once you get used to order, boy, there's no going back," and I've come to appreciate her comment more and more. I live a far from perfectly ordered life, but the order I have achieved I cherish. Becoming neater has a huge effect on mindset, perhaps because neatness has such a strong visual component. If you learn to hang up your bathroom towels neatly, seeing them in a heap or hanging at weird angles from the towel rack is really going to bug you. If you give up your habit of leaving the hall closet open when you grab your coat and instead teach yourself to close it, soon you'll automatically close any gaping closet door or drawer because it just looks *wrong*. That's why driving a microresolution hard, with single-minded purpose, is so critical. It's the relentless practice of your habit that establishes a *new normal* for your mindset.

CHAPTER 14

Relationships

For every action there is an equal and opposite reaction.

—Newton's third law of motion

The relationships we foster with family, partners, friends, and coworkers determine much of our personal happiness and professional success. Relationships are the human channels through which we learn, teach, grow, and become ourselves. Highly dynamic, the tone and balance of a relationship can hinge on something as slender as a passing comment. In a relationship any change to one person affects the other, whether the change is physical, emotional, financial, or linked to an event, such as getting a new job.

So how can just one person in a relationship make a micro-resolution that improves a relationship? *By shifting behavior at the vital margin.* While you may think that your relationship issues involve of necessity *the other guy*, you can't change *the other guy*, you can only change yourself. The good news is that a change in your behavior can, on its own, increase mutual understanding and enjoyment, reduce stress, foster love, build respect, and keep simple disagreements from escalating into painful conflicts. And as the father of physics famously observed, there will be a reaction from *the other guy*, because any change in a relationship dynamic will have reciprocal, if lopsided, effects.

Often we resist changing our own behavior in a relationship because we get hung up on negotiating outcomes that we think are absolutely fair. Relationships aren't generally fair, if by "fair" we mean that everything is *equal*. One partner may do more for the other; one may earn more; one may be more empathetic, energetic, neat, easygoing, outgoing, complacent, successful, compliant, confident, confrontational, righteous, timid, or aggressive. Partners may contribute fully and in good faith to the relationship's health and success, but that doesn't mean that such contributions can be weighed on a scale and brought into perfect balance. It might not be fair that you work to improve your behavior when *the other guy* is mostly to blame, but it might get you to a better place faster than waiting on *the other guy* to improve himself. If your relationship with your mother makes you unhappy, trying to get her to address her shortcomings is probably a longer (and perhaps less productive) road than simply modifying your response to her behavior to reduce friction and achieve a healthier relationship dynamic.

Relationships may not be symmetrical, but they are symbiotic. Disrupting just one negative relationship dynamic can immediately improve your relationship, whether it's at home, at school, at the office, or with a friend or romantic partner. If you pay close attention to how your communication with, investment in, and even thoughts of another person affect you both, you'll identify behavioral patterns that you can improve all on your own.

Self-Expression

I'd been practicing microresolutions for over a year before I made my marriage the target of a microresolution. One night, while apologizing to my husband after he reminded me of something I hadn't done, I realized how much resentment I felt. At the end of a day that included getting my daughter off to school, working eleven demanding hours on Wall Street, and cooking dinner for everyone, his reminder felt unfair—but I rushed to apologize anyway. I followed up my apology with an elaborate explanation of all I *had* done that day.

Apologizing was something I witnessed my mother doing all the time I was growing up. She worked like crazy to keep three kids and a husband on track and happy, yet she apologized regularly for anything she missed. She was the housekeeper, gourmet cook, gardener, psychologist, nurse, laundress, art teacher, tutor, ego booster, and chauffeur. She put herself last, and yet she apologized instantly for anything she failed to do and the few sacrifices she wouldn't make. I think she thought that apologizing was the easiest way to defuse the bad humor of others, but at some level she must have felt angry that, despite being deeply loved by her family, her extraordinary efforts on their behalf weren't fully appreciated.

Here I was, a generation later, a successful working mother, observing in myself the same habit of making needless apologies over trivial issues. Stepping back from my behavior, I realized that my apologies didn't seem to please my husband either; neither one of us felt good after these exchanges. I asked myself what would happen if I just stopped apologizing for the small things I'd missed. What if in response to a reminder or rare admonishment

I didn't say anything or just said, "okay," "yeah," "got it," or "oops"? I decided to give it a try. I resolved:

To stop apologizing to my husband when I didn't really mean it

It wasn't until I tried to stop apologizing that I realized how often I felt the impulse to apologize and then *explain*. But stopping myself from apologizing had an almost magical effect. To begin with, skipping the apology meant I didn't burn a lot of energy defending myself, and I stayed cool and relaxed. Because I didn't apologize falsely, I didn't feel abased or angry, and I could see that most of the small things my husband brought up didn't really require an explanation. I had been responding to his comments as *gotchas*; now I stopped worrying whether or not they were intended as gotchas and just acknowledged them as informational. *If a tree falls in the forest and no one is around to hear it, does it make a sound? If a gotcha doesn't getcha, is it still a gotcha?*

As soon as I stopped explaining myself my resentment dissipated and I realized that my knee-jerk (i.e., autopilot) defensiveness had only served to amplify petty frictions. Simply acknowledging my husband's comment instead of defending myself kept the oxygen from being sucked out of the entire evening and created an opportunity (airtime) for my husband to play down the transaction himself. Where my effusive apologies had mostly been met with stony silence, my new de minimis acknowledgments seemed to prompt my husband to close out the issue himself by saying something like "I know you have a lot on your plate" or "It's no big deal."

Once I rid myself of these gratuitous apologies, I could see that they had been a tactic—my apology was really just an excuse to recite all I had done that my husband should appreciate and make him feel guilty for picking on me. Undoing my habit of instant apology/explanation made me feel lighter, less burdened, because I had let go of some emotional baggage. I became a better half.

The *no bad-faith apologies* pledge is a powerful model for a microresolution focused on self-expression in a relationship. What we say, how we say it, and how we react to emotional cues determine whether or not we are heard and understood and our most personal feelings appreciated. Identifying and changing a negative pattern in self-expression can lead both to a positive shift in a relationship and greater personal authenticity. The first step in achieving progress is to take a close look at how you communicate your needs, thoughts, and support to your opposite number in a relationship.

Engaging on Autopilot

If your goal in a relationship is greater understanding and harmony, analyzing what cues negative engagement is a powerful starting point for a microresolution focused on achieving cleaner, clearer, and more satisfying interactions. In analyzing your reactions to the behavior of others, you might discover that you've fallen into response patterns that impede mutual understanding and personal growth. We may not think of our relationships as governed by autopilot, but guilt-tripping, one-upping, told-you-so-ing, last word–ing, scolding, grudge-holding, snarkism, sarcasm, put-downs, interrupting, defending, complaining, and bossing are all habits that are automatically set in

motion by cues that you don't even realize exist. If you can identify these cues, you can create microresolutions to retrain your
autopilot to respond in a healthier way. Most of these responses,
even the most aggressive ones, are defensive (e.g., being snarky
to a loved one to express hurt feelings without acknowledging
vulnerability). If you examine these reciprocal dynamics in a
particular relationship, you'll discover opportunities to shift
your behavior at the vital margin to achieve a better relationships and a more authentic self.

Shouting Down

Being a parent can be a frustrating experience. We want so
much to be able to help our children, yet we often feel that they
don't hear or respond to our guidance. Although we may sometimes feel tempted to give them a good shake to awaken them
to our message, a breakthrough is more likely if we shake up our
own behavior.

As my daughter approached her teens, I often reacted to her
new rebelliousness with too much heat. This happened if I was
especially frustrated with her behavior or stressed out about
what I perceived to be my own failures as a parent. In such con-
frontations, I would raise my voice repeatedly, intensifying the
battle of wills until we ended up in a loud, tearful standoff.
Thinking through these episodes and how they escalated out of
control, I put on my microresolution thinking cap and decided
to turn my own behavior on its head. I resolved *to lower my
voice* in response to a provocative action or comment by my
daughter. As it turned out, speaking quietly created more inten-
sity than yelling. My points came across as deliberate and serious. If my daughter continued to raise her voice, I lowered mine

further until she had to quiet herself to hear me. This put the focus on the content of what I was saying, rather than on my manner of communication—my yelling had only made it easier for my daughter to dismiss me. My microresolution didn't always carry the day, but it often kept the two of us from going to the brink, it left the lines of communication open, and I felt a lot better about my conduct as a parent.

The ability to respond to the content of a communication rather than to its tone and manner is a very valuable skill, both in and outside the workplace. The emotional style of a communication may be provocative, but what is actually being *said*? If your father's tone is so aggressive when he's telling you how to handle a situation that his advice seems more like an order than a suggestion, it might still be good advice. If you habitually respond with anger or protestations that you're not an idiot or by hanging up the phone, perhaps a microresolution *to always repeat advice given to me by Dad before responding* would give you a chance to hear the advice in your own voice and a neutral tone before responding. Or you might resolve *to thank Dad for his recommendations without giving my own opinion.* Or if you really fear being drawn further into a discussion (or debate), you might resolve *to respond to Dad's advice only by saying, 'You've given me a lot to think about.'* You may never get your dad to express his advice in a way that respects your autonomy and full maturity, so why participate in this emotional grappling? Instead, make a microresolution to respond in a way that puts you in control of your own feelings and self-expression rather than in a way that gets you into an emotional arms race with your parent.

But How Do You Really Feel?

Julia had the habit of second-guessing what others *really* wanted or meant: Wasn't Jenny too busy to come out to dinner but just didn't want to disappoint her? Neil had agreed to join her for a movie but his tone had been cool; should she let him off the hook? Rebecca said she didn't need help, but she seemed so beleaguered; shouldn't she keep offering until Rebecca accepted? In obsessing about how best to gratify the unspoken needs of others, Julia ended up sending mixed signals herself, always giving the other person an "out" after he or she had accepted an invitation, repeatedly offering help to those who said they needed no help, and seeking frequent reassurances that an already-agreed plan was still on. Julia made a microresolution *to take friends at their word.* That meant ignoring possible backstories and perceived emotional atmospherics and simply accepting that what was said was what was meant. Her resolution required that she simply take yes or no for an answer without second-guessing.

Julia found her resolution unbelievably difficult; before she could stop herself she'd offer excuses on the other person's behalf. She tuned her resolution during its first weeks, scaling it back to a single relationship that she used to model her new behavior. With practice, she learned to work through her discomfort and stop herself from doing the thinking for both herself and the other person in the relationship. At that point Julia expanded her microresolution to cover all her social relationships. Did she continue to wonder what *friend X* might really be thinking? Yes, but she didn't act on her insecurity by quizzing her friend about unexpressed feelings; instead she responded based on what he or she had said. In doing so, Julia discovered that the ambivalence she attributed to her friends was often her own, but it wasn't until she stopped fixating on the *real* wishes of others that she could bring her own feelings into focus. Her interactions became more direct and less exhaustive and exhausting. Julia is now considering a microresolution to cover her work relationships, where she realizes she often second-guesses her boss and is overly solicitous of coworkers.

Disappointing Others

Sometimes the fear of disappointing others leads us to express ourselves in dishonest ways. Telling someone that they're not getting promoted is a difficult work communication, and disappointment is to be expected; if you try to spare your worker's feelings by telling him the cause was simply "quotas" or "politics," you're sending a message that his own efforts don't matter, and depriving him of feedback that might contribute to a successful outcome next time. If you are letting an employee go because of poor performance, trying to depersonalize the interaction by blaming the system or shielding him from your reasoning negates your relationship with him and isolates him at a critical moment in his life. Trying to get between a child and his disappointment by convincing him that what he lost wasn't really worth having won't make him feel better or help him to come to grips with one of life's essential realities: You can't always get what you want. If you find that you habitually avoid situations and conversations that may cause disappointment, you might discover, as in the example below, that a microresolution can help you to respond in a more respectful way that creates greater trust.

The Favor of a Reply Is Requested

Alistair was an intelligent and charming person, socially much in demand, who had a terrible time disappointing people, both acquaintances and those close to him. He had trouble declining invitations, discouraging casual get-togethers, or cutting off phone conversations that went on too long. Rather than say no to a solicitation, he put off returning phone calls, and even e-mails went unanswered for weeks. If Alistair was pressed for time and ran into a colleague eager to chat, he escaped by asking him to lunch at a future date, even if he was already overwhelmed by work and social commitments. This habit of avoiding and deferring rather than disappointing created a pile of emotional IOUs that could never be paid off.

Alistair was determined to try to make a change in his behavior, at least in the workplace. He resolved that when he was in a hurry and encountered a chatty colleague, he would not end the conversation by promising to "talk later," "call you," or "have lunch." He forced himself to say that he had to go, was on his way somewhere, or had an appointment and just left it at that. "It's killing me," says Alistair, "but I'm doing it, and it gets a little easier every time. Yesterday I just sort of blurted out I had to run before I had a chance to cringe."

If you're part of a relationship dynamic that you'd like to improve, think about the circumstances that cue your negative behavior and come up with a microresolution that replaces a negative response pattern with a constructive one. When your mother talks about your brother's brilliant career, does it lead you to try to take your brother down a peg? What would happen if you resolved to match everything your mother said about your brother with something equally nice, or just calmly went on to a different topic, or resolved never to make an accusation of favoritism? (Honestly, what does it get you?) When your partner tells you he or she will be home at a certain hour and he or she is an hour late, do you respond with the silent treatment, ruining what's left of the evening? What would happen if you greeted your partner warmly and committed yourself to an enjoyable evening anyway? When a coworker who is less competent comes to you for help, do you make sure that the boss knows it later? How might your relationship to the entire team and your own leadership improve if you resolved not to promote yourself by mentioning such incidents to the boss? Once you realize that you yourself can disrupt an ingrained relationship pattern by making a shift in your own behavior, you'll be able to devise microresolutions that make a real difference with family, romantic partners, friends, and work colleagues.

On the Job

Success at work can depend heavily on the quality of your relationships—with your boss, coworkers, reports, clients, and customers. Building strong relationships boosts your effectiveness and creates a valuable network to support you throughout your working life. One poor relationship at work can threaten your success, render your efforts on the job less effective, and cast a pall over your entire working day.

As discussed at the outset of this chapter, if you find yourself in a work relationship that needs improving, focusing on the shortfalls of *the other guy* won't lead to a breakthrough. But changing just one behavior of your own—a tendency to interrupt, complain, dismiss, or defend—can put your relationship on a healthier track.

Let Me Finish

After many years in the same managerial position, Christine moved into a new job that she thought represented a great opportunity. Her new assignment came with a new boss, her first after years of working for a manager who had been both a mentor and a close friend. Christine's new boss had an aggressive manner and was more likely to fault than praise. And he had a communication habit that drove her nuts: During their one-on-one meetings he interrupted her whenever he thought he knew what she was going to say. If he got it wrong and Christine persisted in clarifying her point, he seemed to feel one-upped, and she felt frustrated that she wasn't able to communicate her efforts and achievements clearly.

Christine felt her boss's impatience was rude, but after several weeks she accepted that his behavior wasn't likely to change. She began thinking through how she might adjust her own behavior so that she and her boss didn't end up wrangling over punch lines. Christine made a microresolution to create a briefing paper to send to her boss the night before their weekly meeting. Preparing the brief would be extra work, but it would give her a chance to make her points without a fight. She included a bold headline for every topic in the brief, so that if her boss didn't read the details he could still see where she was headed. Christine was sorry to give up the informal meeting style that had been so productive with her previous manager, but she felt she had to make a change if she was to create a better communication dynamic with her new boss.

The briefing notes transformed the meeting and made it feel less competitive. Christine's boss could get straight to the issues he thought merited most attention, and their discussions took off, becoming both shorter and more productive. In the aftermath Christine realized that she had been so eager to show her new boss all that she had been doing and thinking that he had become impatient with the meeting pace. She had been using the meeting to review her work rather than as a springboard for making decisions. Preparing the brief gave her the chance to demonstrate all her thinking and actions without bogging down the discussion.

Christine's microresolution made her time with the boss really productive, but it's important to emphasize the habits that had to be created to make it work. The first time she sent her boss the brief she raised his expectations that there would always be a brief sent the night before the meeting, and showing up without it would have counted as a fail. Introducing the brief meant institutionalizing it, and it required practice and discipline to make an absolute routine of it.

Viral Self-Improvement

Simon was given an assignment to begin managing a team that was underperforming and had suffered defections of team members to other projects and companies. The team had an entrenched, depleted atmosphere, confidence was low, and the team was facing a difficult project schedule.

Simon understood that to be successful he would have to lift the team's performance by turning around underperformers or by replacing them. He knew that his reputation as an aggressive manager had preceded him and saw that his new team viewed him warily. While he was committed to taking tough actions to turn the team around, he began thinking about his own behavior and what he might do differently to win the trust of the team and foster a culture of excellence.

If he wanted others to improve, Simon reasoned, he would have to demonstrate that he viewed developmental feedback as a personal opportunity. Simon made a microresolution to end biweekly face-to-face meetings with each of his new managers by asking for feedback on what he could be doing better. The first few times he asked for their feedback, his managers were either mostly vague or made only positive comments. Simon persisted in his resolution, and his reports soon began coming prepared to give direct feedback. Prompted by his example, most of his direct reports began asking Simon for developmental feedback, allowing him to engage team leaders about performance shortfalls in a natural and positive way. Following the pattern established by Simon, many of his managers began asking their teams for feedback, prompting deeper conversations about what needed to change and creating an atmosphere of open collegiality and collaboration. Soon a culture of continuous engagement, feedback, and problem solving took hold, and the team began to improve. While Simon did replace some people on the team for poor performance, most of the original team survived, and in nine months the team was humming.

Why Me?

Although Greta was a good person who enjoyed a good time, she had a habit of complaining. She complained about trivial episodes on transit, at work, and at merchants—the bus that didn't stop when the driver clearly saw her running for it, the butcher who gave her loin rather than rib lamb chops, the salesclerk who pressured her into buying something she didn't really want.

Greta was a hard worker, very skilled and conscientious, but if she had to work late, pick up the slack for an absent employee, or miss lunch, she complained about it. She wasn't a person of ill will; her complaints were mostly a misguided attempt to bond with other employees and to feel a greater sense of belonging (we're all powerless together).

After Greta received feedback that she wasn't being promoted to a more senior spot because her negative attitude wasn't right for a leadership position, she began to take stock. Her first impulse was to feel that she had been treated unfairly, as her general resentment was a defensive posture. But looking back over her career, she could see a pattern in her attitude and behavior that she decided needed serious attention.

Greta's first microresolution was *I will not to be the first to complain about a work issue.* The very first day of her resolution, something happened in the office that she thought worthy of complaint. In accordance with her resolution, she made no comment and instead waited eagerly for someone else to bitch. She recalls, "I thought to myself, *Here it comes, here it comes, wait for it!*—and nothing happened. No one said a thing!" It was days before anyone voiced a mild complaint on a different topic. "It was me," Greta said. "I never realized that I was at the core of the complaining; it seemed to be a general thing. But when I stopped taking the lead, most of it died off."

Greta's pledge *not to complain first* is a classic example of working the vital margin. Greta didn't pledge *never to complain again under any circumstances*; instead her target was limited, reasonable, and, as it turned out, revelatory.

If you have the habit of complaining at work, you might try a resolution that places some limits on your complaining. For example, you might resolve to give up complaining about a certain topic (coworkers, boss, work assignments, hours) or limit whom you complain to (for example, *I resolve to complain about work only at home*) or limit when you complain (*I resolve not to complain at lunch or on coffee breaks*).

If you're a complainer in your personal life, you might resolve to give up a single (boring) category of complaint entirely, such as traffic/transit/travel, disappointing food, the weather, minor health issues, petty work grievances, life's necessary errands/chores, or minor disses you've suffered. Narrowing your resolution to a very specific target you know you can achieve is the key to making your behavioral shift stick. Reversing the complaining habit will be hard work, since complaining is a kind of self-comfort. So think fearlessly about a change in behavior that will have a positive impact, and work it.

Listening to a chronic complainer turns out to be more than just annoying, it's actually bad for your brain. New research conducted at Friedrich Schiller University in Germany demonstrated that being on the receiving end of complaining can have a negative effect on your brain, outlook, and ability to solve problems.* If you play the role of ear to a chronic complainer at work or in your personal life, think about a microresolution that will shake up the dynamic so that you don't end up absorbing all that negativity.

Call Me Maybe

Mei often responded to issues raised by clients, colleagues, and subordinates through e-mails. She found communicating asynchronously convenient to her work schedule and less stressful

---

* Thomas Straube, Andreas Sauer, and Wolfgang H. R. Miltner, "Brain Activation During Direct and Indirect Processing of Positive and Negative Words," *Behavioural Brain Research* 222, no. 1 (September 12, 2011): 66–72.

than in-person or phone communication, especially if there were issues to resolve. But her lengthy e-mail responses led to hardened positions more often than to better understanding. After one such exchange blew up with a client and caused an intervention by her boss, Mei thought about her habit of conducting most of her client business through e-mail. She made a microresolution that if an issue didn't get resolved after one brief e-mail exchange, she would pick up the phone and call her correspondent. Calling up a colleague or client and saying, "I saw your e-mail. Shall we talk it through together?" is much more disarming than sending a "no need to worry because you have it all wrong" e-mail, and some of the conversations ended with a simple "Never mind!" within sixty seconds. It's worth emphasizing that making a commitment to take disagreements out of e-mail *every time* takes discipline and practice before the impulse to type is replaced by the impulse to dial. Examining the role a communication channel—e-mail, text, phone, chat, social media, face to face—plays in a relationship dynamic might reveal an opportunity to make a change that leads to more productive exchanges.

The skill, creativity, and dedication you bring to the performance of your job is the greatest predictor of your success, whether your job is tending bar, managing a newsroom, or nursing people back to health. But the success of your relationships at work will also determine your effectiveness and how your job performance is perceived: your ability to work with a positive attitude and as a productive member of a team, manage diverse relationships in a healthy and professional manner, communicate effectively with others, and lead with integrity. Changing a key behavior or attitude through a microresolution can improve your job performance, satisfaction, and career prospects.

MICRORESOLUTIONS IN ACTION

Being There

I once attended a master class given by Stella Adler, Marlon Brando's acting teacher, where I heard her say to an actor struggling to play a character in love, "How can you tell when a someone is in love? How can you tell? You can tell because they *pay attention*. They pay attention to their lover's every action, gesture, and expression. So," she continued to the actor (and the entire room), "if you're playing someone in love, give the love object your complete attention in a scene. Even if you aren't looking at your lover directly, even if you're talking to another character, you are *always paying attention*. Everything the love object does should fascinate you."

What's the quality of your attention when you finally make time for an important relationship? Do you check your cell phone for updates when you're out with your kid and immediately respond to even noncritical e-mails as he chomps down his grilled cheese in silence? Do you multitask on the computer while carrying on a phone conversation with a parent? If your girlfriend comes into a room and sighs, do you pretend not to have heard her through your earbuds? Do you space out as soon as your spouse begins telling you details of a hobby or work project but make grunts at intervals to indicate active listening? In short, do you pay attention, or do you phone it in?

Our multitasking, asynchronous, headlines-only, emoticon culture can erode communication and connection in even our most cherished relationships. Yet just as you learned to understand and communicate in texts consisting of four misspelled words and a face made out of a colon and a parenthesis mark, you can retrain yourself through microresolutions to pay better attention to the relationships that matter most, when it matters most.

Out of Pocket

A divorced dad of two budding teenagers, Alex wanted to make the weekends he had with the kids count. He moved out of the city and into a community of rustic weekend houses that share one thousand acres of hiking trails, lakes, and horseback riding. The idea was to create a second home with distinct advantages over the life the children lived in Manhattan.

During the first weekend in the house, the kids spent plenty of time on their phones, talking and texting with friends, exploring apps, and playing games. While the kids occupied themselves with their electronics, Alex caught up on work on his computer. After he dropped the kids at school Monday morning, he realized that although they had spent the entire weekend together, they hadn't had the kind of experience that the move to the country was supposed to make possible. What was the point of gathering together in a wonderful setting if all three of them just enjoyed their electronics severally? So in the two weeks leading up to their next weekend together, Alex resolved *to limit cell-phone time on weekend days to an hour*. When he told the kids about the new rule, there were vehement protests. "What do I tell my friends?" demanded his highly social preteen daughter. "Tell them your dad's a jerk!" (or similar), he replied. Alex collected the cell phones and gave them back each day at 5:00 p.m. for an hour. The weekends became about going outside to swim, ride, or hike. In the evenings they read, played board games (!), or watched a movie together. The grousing about the phones stopped. And Alex himself kept to the rule, staying off the phone for all but the most important business calls. The house in the woods did indeed become the special place he had envisioned for his children.

Rerun

Fran had a demanding job and went to bed earlier than her husband, Ted, whose work kept him up long past midnight. Ted often kept the television on in the background, sometimes watching a late movie at the end of the night when he ran out of creative steam. He liked to recap these movies to Fran, which she found extremely boring, such boredom expressed in lack of eye contact, fidgeting, and sighing. But despite the lack of interest she showed, Ted continued to tell her about the movies. Since he was going to tell her anyway, Fran reasoned, she might as well make him feel good about it by responding with more interest. She resolved *to give Ted my complete attention when he tells me about a movie*. Rather than busying herself with something as her husband recounted the previous night's movie, Fran kept eye contact as he talked and even asked questions. While she says she never really got much more interested, the warmth her attention created was palpable. "I'm honestly surprised," says Fran, "how much goodwill was created between us just by my sitting down and giving him my complete attention when he told me about a movie. The whole thing only took five minutes, where when I was trying to discourage him from telling me it seemed like forever. And I realized something else once I stopped resisting—I had felt resentful that Ted's work allowed him to stay up late and watch films, when I have to get up so early."

Paying attention makes loved ones and work colleagues feel valued. While it's impossible to pay close attention to another person all the time (posthoneymoon, anyway), picking up the most important bids for attention (cues) can work wonders. If your partner has a special project or hobby, you might resolve to show particular interest whenever it comes up (isolate the cue), rather than just nodding in an absent way while waiting to engage on a topic that interests you.

Making Time

It's hard to pay attention to people if you're always too busy to spend time with them.

Time in a day is a zero-sum game—you can't make more of it, so it's really all about priorities. Most of your time is managed by autopilot, where the priorities are baked in. You may not think much about spending two hours reading the newspaper on Sundays, but if you do it regularly, it's a top priority. If you spend time surfing the Internet every evening or vegging out for a few hours of reality TV, those are the priorities you've established for your time. If a relationship you'd like to improve wants attention, examine how you might change your habits to free up more time for it.

Many of us count on the weekends for catching up with others and devoting time to personal interests. Yet the weekend, which from the vantage point of Monday appears as a lavish, solid block of free time, by Saturday morning reveals itself to be limited and fragmented. If you cheat on sleep throughout the week, you may sleep away half of Saturday and stumble through the rest of the day at half throttle. Add to that miscalculation the burden of myriad chores and obligations that collect throughout the week, and it's easy to find yourself wondering on Sunday night how it was you didn't manage to find time for an outing with a partner, friend, or child or a single hour to pursue a personal interest.

Using microresolutions to help you get more sleep during the week (see chapter 10, "Sleep") so that you don't waste half the weekend recharging will release some time that you can spend on yourself or others. Ditto creating habits that keep administrative work from becoming an oppressive pile that can be dispensed only via a marathon weekend session (see chapter 17, "Organization").

Another way to increase the time you have for nurturing relationships is to convert a solo activity (on weekdays or weekends) into an opportunity to spend time with someone. Walking to work with a colleague; working out with a friend; establishing a monthly lunch with a subordinate; doing laundry with your girlfriend; going to the green market with a parent; doing your own homework at the kitchen table alongside your kid—examine how you spend your days and see if you can commit to a microresolution that creates a new opportunity for sharing and connection.

Kitchen Confidential

For years my routine on returning home from work was to check in with the *fam* and then get straight on to making the evening meal. I put pressure on myself to get dinner on the table at a reasonable hour, that pressure increasing if I made a late exit from work. As revealed by my personal anecdotes in the book, I'm a speedy multitasker, and nowhere is this more evident than in the kitchen, where my actions resemble those of a Benihana chef minus the grace and entertainment value. When my husband came into the kitchen to hang out, I'd tell him I'd rather visit during dinner. But dinner was the three of us, and much of the time after dinner was absorbed by homework and bedtime routines. My husband and I often didn't have a chance to visit alone until late in the evening, when we were most depleted.

In trying to alter my habits to create more weeknight time with my husband, I made a microresolution to hang with him during dinner prep, even if it slowed dinner down. It took me a while after making this resolution to relax my approach enough to enjoy visiting with him while I was making dinner. Dinner did indeed end up taking about ten minutes longer to prepare, but in exchange for this minor delay I gained around forty minutes of early-evening time with my husband. The whole dinner hour was more relaxed since my husband and I had already synced up on our days and discussed any pressing issues before we sat down to eat as a family. Rushing to make dinner and stressing myself out about timing was a habit that I had to work consciously to unwind; now I can't imagine anything more pleasant than chatting with my husband while cooking the family meal.

Trust

Many relationship issues, in both public and private life, come down to trust. "Honesty is the best policy" we learn from the elementary-school history of George Washington, but few of us practice this principle in the purest sense. Telling the absolute truth in every situation may not be the best policy, but how many of us manipulate the truth as a routine matter of convenience? For example, do we really need to make up an intricate excuse to get out of a date, or can we just cancel and say that we are sorry to do so? If we're late to work, do we have to tell an elaborate story about the perils of public transit? If a friend asks us for an honest opinion about a life issue, should we hide or shade the truth in order to tell them what they want to hear? Sparing feelings can get to be a habit, a modus operandi for dealing with any less-than-pleasant topic, and it's not always easy to know whether we're protecting ourselves or another person when we are less than truthful in our communications. A microresolution can help you shift your relationship habits in a more truthful direction and create more trust.

There's a famous *I Love Lucy* episode* where Lucy, reproached by Desi, Ethel, and Fred for her pathological fibbing, bets them a hundred dollars that she can tell the absolute truth for twenty-four hours. The struggle to keep her resolution intensifies rapidly as Lucy confronts how often she shades the truth, exaggerates, or tells white lies just to get through the day. When she and Ethel visit their friend Carolyn's apartment to play bridge, they find she has recently redecorated with Chinese-modern furniture. With Carolyn out of earshot, Lucy looks around and remarks to Ethel, "Looks like a bad dream you'd have after eating too much Chinese food." On reentering, Carolyn asks Lucy point-blank whether or not she likes her new furniture. Lucy, chafing under her resolution, threads the needle by replying, "Uh, I said *it looked like a dream*, didn't I, Ethel?" Ethel, a party to the bet, sees her chance and demands that Lucy give a verbatim account of her remark. Unwilling to lose her wager, Lucy comes clean, shocking her old friend. Next Lucy grapples with the arrival of Marian, the bridge game's fourth, who is sporting a hideous new hat. Goaded once again by Ethel to express her true thoughts, Lucy confesses that she thinks the hat "is the silliest I've ever seen" and, when pressed further, "horrible."

The truth-telling stakes quickly advance from the dangers of

---

* "Lucy Tells the Truth," DesiLu productions, 1953.

offending others to that of self-exposure. The three women gang up on Lucy and try to force her into losing the bet by demanding to know her age, weight, and true hair color. Cornered, an identity crisis upon her, Lucy is momentarily frozen, agape at the cruelty of her friends' opportunism. Then something relaxes inside Lucy and she fires off the answers to all three questions, "33, 129, and mousy brown," suddenly converting her vulnerability into strength. The cozy bridge club gasps at Lucy's daring in revealing such closely guarded feminine secrets (episode year: 1953). Briskly dealing out cards to her stunned friends, Lucy declares, "I feel very relieved. It's wonderful to tell the truth! You should try it sometime; we'd all be much better friends!" Exhilarated by her newfound freedom to speak her mind, Lucy clears the air of old business by calling out her bridge partners for cheating, excessive yakking, and being too cheap to replace a filthy deck of playing cards. As Marian laughs uncontrollably at the truths meted to others, Lucy exclaims, "Stop that cackling, Marian. I've been waiting ten years for you to lay that egg."

While Lucy's bet is a situational device designed to create comedic opportunities, it does share some of a microresolution's attributes. Lucy's resolution is a specific and measurable action, limited to a single day, and Lucy believes that it's an *easy* resolution that can be executed with no excuses.

How does Lucy's proto-microresolution stack up to rule 3, "A microresolution pays off up front"? Although Lucy ultimately loses the bet when she lies in order to compete for a showbiz opportunity, she has clearly gained something invaluable through her resolution. The audience witnesses a liberated Lucy discovering the power of communicating honestly, rather than artfully, with her friends (and later that evening with her husband). Although her resolution to tell the truth ends after a day, it's impossible to believe that Lucy hasn't changed for the better forever. By treating her loved ones to the "Full Lucy," she comes in closer contact with her authentic power as a human being. Breaking the tired pattern of deceptive communication changes the dynamic of the bridge club for more than just a day, since the four women have discovered that it is possible to deal honestly with one another, reveal personal secrets, and still remain friends.

I'm not suggesting that you tell your friend you hate her hat; we don't have to go as far as Lucy to learn how to communicate more honestly. A microresolution that results in being more truthful in a circumstance where we habitually shade or avoid the truth can create new opportunities to connect genuinely with friends, family, and coworkers. Like Lucy, we may begin with fear of revealing too much, but as we get the hang of more authentic communication, we too may find ourselves "relieved" to deal more truthfully with others and exhilarated to come in contact with a truer and more powerful self.

Relationships that run into serious trouble may require professional attention, but for the most part you don't need a high summit, professional arbitration, or a come-to-Jesus meeting to make a relationship breakthrough. Focusing on your own behavior rather than on the behavioral issues of others builds maturity and integrity and promotes personal growth. Resolving to disrupt just one negative behavior pattern in a relationship will have a positive effect on both the relationship and your sense of self. While many of our good and bad qualities have psychological roots that could take a lifetime to fully understand, resolving to change a single behavior, even in a narrow context, can prove revelatory and personally transforming.

When we improve the way we habitually respond to others, we advance ourselves as human beings. Over two thousand years ago in ancient Greece, Aristotle taught that character results not from being but doing:

> Men acquire a particular quality by constantly acting in a particular way. . . . You become just by performing just actions, temperate by performing temperate actions, brave by performing brave actions.

CHAPTER 15

Spending

> Annual income twenty pounds, annual expenditure
> nineteen pounds nineteen and six, result happiness. An-
> nual income twenty pounds, annual expenditure twenty
> pounds ought and six, result misery.
>
> —Charles Dickens, *David Copperfield*

There are a great number of good financial books and advisers to teach you how to budget, invest, and plan to reach long-term financial goals. *Small Move, Big Change* is not a substitute for such a book or for professional financial advice. But spending behaviors and attitudes are part of your autopilot; indeed, your lifestyle is a matter of unconscious routine. Using microresolutions to improve your spending mindset and habits at the margin can help you keep your expenditures aligned with your long-term financial goals.

Spending patterns are a reflection of priorities, whether or not you have consciously considered them. Your dollars are like votes you cast at different retail and investment ballot boxes. So many votes for housing, energy, food, dining out, entertainment, cable TV, mobile, clothing, electronics, vacations, savings, mutual funds.

Do you know what you've elected as your spending priorities? The very first step in getting more from your earnings is to understand where your money is going now, so that you can identify the marginal spending behaviors impeding your financial goals.

Thirsting for Savings

Yolanda and Jan, both well-paid professionals, analyzed their spending patterns for opportunities to save money. They scrutinized the relatively high cost of dining out, yet both felt these restaurant evenings worth preserving. Was there another, related expenditure they could target for savings instead? After examining their combined spending habits on food and snacks, Yolanda and Jan each made a microresolution *to stop buying bottled soft drinks*. That meant no designer water, commercial iced teas, or sodas. With each of them forgoing three drinks a day, this single resolution saved them close to four hundred dollars a month (folks, this is New York City). Yolanda and Jan also liked that their new habit cut down on recycling and reduced their consumption of empty calories. Their success is a perfect example of an individualized spending resolution that makes an impact by reforming an autopilot behavior that had never before attracted any notice. There are hundreds of expenditures you make each month as a matter of habit that you can eliminate or curtail to improve your bottom line. But start with one!

Convenience Is Expensive

When I finally took a hard look at my own spending patterns, I could clearly see that I placed a premium on speed (cue theme music) and convenience. In our hardworking world, the lure of doing what is easiest and fastest often separates us from our money. It's faster to take a cab than to ride the bus; easier to pick something up at the expensive grocery next door than to walk six blocks to the supermarket; faster to buy the name-brand item than to research high-value, low-cost alternatives; faster to park in an illegal zone for just ten minutes and risk (another) ticket than to park farther away. If you wait until the last minute to send holiday gifts or to book airline tickets, it will cost you. If you don't cancel appointments and classes within the allowable time period, you'll have to pay a penalty. Laziness is expensive, I realized, and I decided to change my ways.

My first spending microresolution was *to have zero tolerance for withdrawing money from an ATM that charged a fee.* I used to withdraw money from the most convenient location, rather than walking a few blocks out of my way to avoid the fee. I told myself that the time saved was worth a couple of bucks. But ATM fees in New York range from two to three dollars per withdrawal; for every withdrawal of a hundred dollars, you're paying 2 to 3 percent on after-tax income! That's more than the interest you get on savings, more than any tax hike contemplated by Congress! As with any change in routine brought on by a microresolution, it irked me to change my habit of going to the cash machine on the ground floor of my office building, and I had to force myself to walk the extra blocks; now I can't stand the idea that I might find myself in an emergency situation where I would be compelled to pay this ridiculous fee. Change your habit, change your head. Once I became fanatic about not forking over the ATM fee, I started obsessing about other needless fees I might be paying.

Automatic payments and electronic bills are a great convenience and useful in ensuring obligations are paid on time, but if you've fallen out of the habit of reviewing monthly charges, you are probably overpaying, in some cases significantly. Fees are everywhere in the financial world, from late fees to extra charges on your mortgage bill to fees for services you seldom use or may not even need. Misbillings are rampant—I had only just finished getting charges that should have been covered by my calling plan removed from my phone bill when I went home to visit my father and discovered that he too was paying for every phone call *plus* a monthly charge for all-you-can-eat. The extra pages in your bills that look like advertising often contain information about service charge changes and rules that you should read, not toss (or scroll past). If you make a microresolution *to review bills and account statements in detail on the fifteenth of each month*, you'll establish dedicated time to go through statements and charges to make sure you know what you are paying for. Any questionable bills that come up you can toss into the file for review day. During your review session you have only one task: to review monthly bills and bank accounts for unexpected fees or activities and take action.

Unless you have the habit of regularly checking your banking statements, you may be paying subscription fees without knowing it. Many services on the Internet are subscription based; if you once signed up to gain access to something you needed in the short run, chances are you've been paying in the long run. I once agreed to a free trial for creating a post office at home, tried it, didn't like it, and didn't realize until tax time when I reviewed my checking-account statements that when the free trial ended a monthly charge of $15.99 had automatically kicked in. Did I complain? Yes. Did I get my money back? Only for the two months preceding the logging of my complaint; most companies limit refunds to "current charges"—at most a quarter—so that inattention cost me over $175. Don't let the convenience of automatic payments and subscription renewals lull you into wasting money; figure out how often you need to pay attention, and make a resolution that bakes it into your routine. Or make a microresolution to look at your bank account online every day, as my friend Wendy does—she can't bear to go through a monthly statement, but spending three minutes online every day is manageable, and she catches questionable entries right away.

The ultimate example of accepting personal inconvenience in order to save money comes from the childhood of my friend Adam. With three children to raise and educate in New York City, Adam's parents made careful management of money family policy. No expense was too small to attract scrutiny. Adam's parents would make the kids call Information from a pay phone on the street corner because 411 was free from the booth but twenty-five cents from home. Adam's mother would take a route around the Henry Hudson Bridge that added fifteen minutes to the car ride in order to avoid paying the ten-cent toll. She improved on Benjamin Franklin's aphorism that "a penny saved is a penny earned"; by her lights, "a penny saved is more than a penny earned because you've already paid the taxes on it."

Not only did Adam's parents put all three kids through graduate school, but they also live in a superb apartment, have a vacation home and a healthy investment portfolio, and are generous to their children, their friends, and society. They simply didn't want to waste a dime on anything that didn't really improve the quality of their lives. Adam tells me that his parents taught him that it wasn't important to have a new car, only a safe car, and that eating in the best restaurants didn't matter, but the pleasure of a family outing did. Not surprisingly, Adam is a saver, not a spender, has an excellent quality of life, is very secure, and has brunch with his parents every Sunday. In the two decades of our friendship in Manhattan, I can't recall a single occasion where Adam agreed with me that taking a cab was a good idea.

Being a Passive Consumer Is Expensive

Being passive with respect to financial obligations is costly. We're programmed to fall into patterns to save mental energy, but it pays to pay attention when it comes to routine outlays if you're trying to improve your bottom line. Any favorable marginal change to the basic services that form your budget baseline creates renewable savings. Most of us just assume that we're helpless when it comes to what we pay for utilities, cable, and cell phones, when in fact these marketplaces are dynamic and more competitive than ever, creating an opportunity to achieve renewable monthly savings that are significant.

Jody made a microresolution *to research at least one bill for potential savings on the first Saturday in the calendar quarter.* She made a list of all the monthly bills that were part of her baseline spending: phone (land and mobile), energy, house cleaner, garden maintenance, cable, parking, security monitoring, etc. When "bill research" day rolled around each quarter, she'd select a bill to target and go to work. In researching her energy bill, Jody realized for the first time that due to deregulation she was now able to select an independent energy supplier, rather than being locked in to purchasing from her current energy-delivery company. She began researching different suppliers on the Internet, many of which offered guaranteed pricing for two years and gift cards or other promotions. Coming to a decision required Jody to understand how energy is billed, the average amount she paid per energy unit, and the consequences of billing leveling; she had to speak with different energy sales representatives. She couldn't get this all done in her initial session, but as she was clearly on the road to making some savings, she scheduled more time to follow through. Jody swapped out her current energy supplier for fixed pricing for two years. The very first application of her microresolution saved 30 percent off her energy bill.

New opportunities for saving on basic bills emerge all the time: new competitors, billing plans, and consumer options to eliminate waste. Better cell-phone rates and bundled services can lower your monthly bill significantly; reexamining services such as storage, cleaning, maintenance, parking, and personal services may surface new possibilities to make savings. Don't let yourself be paralyzed by all these opportunities and the knowledge that you could probably be doing better; use a microresolution to zero in on one prospect at a time. It could be once a quarter or once a month. It takes time and energy to bring about a change in billing—comparing rates, plans, vendors; reading the fine print on Web sites; waiting in a queue to speak to a representative. If you decide to make a push to reduce your monthly expenditures, make a microresolution that schedules one or two hours a month exclusively for this activity, and stick with the schedule. Remember: limited and easy.

Inspired by Jody's energy-savings success, I resolved to spend two hours a month investigating new opportunities to save on monthly billings, and so far I've changed my energy-delivery company, gotten rid of an outdoor maintenance service, closed down a storage space, replaced some of my one-on-one exercise sessions with group classes, reduced my insurance bill, and consolidated our mobile plans with one carrier. And do we really need all those cable channels?

The great thing about reducing monthly charges is that the savings are renewable. Trimming or eliminating just one monthly charge can add up to considerable savings over time.

Identifying savings and following through with making a change requires a regular investment of time to identify opportunities, execute on them, and track results.

Impulsiveness Is Expensive

The art of retailing is enticing a consumer into an unplanned purchase. Malls and stores are specifically designed to boost impulse spending. Decorations, events, samples, specials, coupons, promotions, unexpected discounts, and clever product displays at checkout are all calculated to get you to spend beyond the limited purpose of your visit. The retailer's goal is to get you to swipe your card before you have a chance to think rationally about the value or affordability of the shiny object dangling in front of you.

A December 2012 survey conducted by the Checkout[*] found that nine out of ten shoppers succumb to impulse purchases. And according to Harris Interactive Polling,[†] 71 percent of survey respondents regretted their impulse purchases even twelve months later, demonstrating that a hasty decision can have a long tail. The regretted impulse purchases broke down as 47 percent apparel, 37 percent dining out, 21 percent children's toys, 21 percent technology, and 7 percent vacations.

If you're prone to impulse buying, you might consider a microresolution that will make you less susceptible to retailer come-ons. Shopping when you're tired or suffering from

---

[*] "Shopping Lists," *The Checkout* 2 (2012).
[†] John Aidan Byrne, "Impulse Buying Has Its Price," *New York Post*, December 10, 2012.

"decision fatigue"* after a long day makes you vulnerable to overspending. You might resolve to limit certain kinds of shopping to the morning hours, when you're least depleted, or to avoid shopping during periods when battling crowds and traffic exhausts your spirit and makes you more susceptible to a spontaneous purchase. You might consider a resolution to wait twenty-four hours before parting with money for an expensive item of a particular type. Stepping back from a transaction and interrupting the momentum of an impulse purchase will help you regain perspective. There's a kind of high in handing over your money and running out of the store with your prize before you have a chance to think better of it (much like gobbling down a treat snatched from a passing tray).

Internet and mobile retailing focus heavily on encouraging impulse buys. The purchases conclude so quickly—just a click—that you often splurge before thinking twice. *Click* to buy this new music album; *click* to get this book that's like the other book you liked so much; now that you're in range of Neiman Marcus, here's a special store coupon you can take inside—just *click*! Social networking sites make it easy to keep up with the purchases and the "likes" of friends and near friends and nonfriends. The global village, now a reality, often seems more like a global mall, lit up and open for business 24/7, ready and waiting whenever the buying impulse strikes. You might resolve not to make any purchase on your phone that you didn't initiate yourself, so that owning a phone does not increase opportunities for impulse buying during the day. Use your phone to make planned expenditures, and if an item is presented for purchase that interests

---

* Kathleen D. Vohs et al., "Making Choices Impairs Subsequent Self-Control: A Limited-Resource Account of Decision Making, Self-Regulation, and Active Initiative," *Journal of Personality and Social Psychology* 94, no. 5 (May 2008): 883–98.

you but that you didn't initiate, don't make the purchase in the moment; make a microresolution to do it from your computer later. In the intervening time, you may lose all interest.

Among my most successful spending microresolutions was to *give up personal shopping on the Internet after 9:30 p.m.* I was particularly vulnerable to browsing online late at night, an expensive entertainment in terms of both money and sleep. My willpower and reason ebbing at day's end, I seldom concluded my sessions without buying something. When the boxes arrived, I couldn't always remember what I had bought. Driving a stake through the heart of my late-night shopping habit has saved me a bundle. I still shop on the Internet (couldn't live without it), but I no longer make late-night personal purchases.

If you regularly have occasion to regret your impulse buys, start by examining the situations that cue you to overspend. For instance, you could make a microresolution *not to spend in order to receive a discount*, thereby eliminating all those situations where you're offered a discount coupon to be used later if you spend more now. In doing so you will keep yourself from overspending today and likely avoid unwise spending in the future prompted only by the notion that you should take advantage of that (expensive) discount coupon. If items at the checkout counter speak to you, a microresolution *to have zero tolerance for adding to the shopping cart once in line to pay* will keep you from scooping up chocolates, magazines, toys, gadgets, and joke books in the final moments of your store visit. In making your resolution, aim to circumvent situations that cause you to lose perspective. That could be shopping with a particular friend, browsing in a particular store, attending frenzied sample sales where elbowing competition creates the notion that there are actually items worth fighting for in the bin. Spending habits are personal and so closely tied to mood that for some it's nearly an addiction. Working to reverse destructive spending patterns means carefully identifying cues and reforming habitual responses.

Waste Is Expensive

Losing sunglasses, a glove, a paid pass, or a watch due to a worn strap that could easily have been replaced is expensive and demoralizing. Items such as reading glasses, mobile phones, and umbrellas are regularly left in restaurants, on public transit, and in cabs. I used to lose three pairs of sunglasses a year until I made a microresolution to always return my sunglasses to the case immediately upon removal. I'm too embarrassed to say how much this resolution has saved me annually, but it is well worth putting in an IRA. Now I've had the same boring pair of sunglasses for three years, but that's a better problem.

It's easy to waste money on clothing that isn't suitable and can't be returned. If you talk yourself into believing that a great pair of boots on sale will stretch a size after wearing them, you won't be able to get your money back even if they cripple you. Buying clothes that you expect to diet into or that require major alterations will probably just lead to lost hanger space in your closet. A friend of mine sends herself the following microresolution message when tempted to shell out for an item that has potential but requires some adjustments: *Stop talking yourself into it and pass.* Remember, the exclusive target of a microresolution message is mindset, and the only measure of its success is that you remembered to send yourself the message on cue (in this case, considering how a clothing item could be modified to work). It might not be wise to make a microresolution *never to buy anything that needs alteration*, because you might run across something that needs so little adjustment and is so fabulous and well priced that it represents a real find. The microresolution message is less absolute, while implanting the attitude that most purchases that require effort and advanced visualization skills are probably losers.

I used to repeatedly get stuck with nonreturnable items from Internet purchases because I failed to act until the window for return had closed. Busy all day and tired at night, I'd push the boxes under the bed and discover them again weeks later—alas, too late to get my money back. I resolved to open boxes only if I had the time to prepare a return immediately in the event I decided not to keep the item. That meant being prepared to print and fill out the form, repack the item, and address the box. Since it's easy to drop off the boxes once they're packed up, I haven't gotten stuck with an item since I made my resolution.

There are many mindless ways to waste resources, from leaving lights and heat on when you leave home, to paying for an expensive second cocktail to be social, to ordering expensive water and espresso as part of lunch. Most wastefulness is mindless habit; examining your own behavior for opportunities to make a change in behavior is the place to start.

Relative Expenditure Is Expensive

Considering expenditures on a relative rather than absolute basis can lead to irrational decisions. For example, if you decide you can afford to spend $1,000 renting a vacation house for a week, it's a small leap to begin looking at houses that cost $1,100/

week. From there it's easy to creep up the cost ladder because each time you look at something more expensive, you're raising the ante by only a *relatively* small amount. You may never have intended to pay $1,500/week, but you end up paying that by creeping up the relative expense ladder.

You need only visit eBay to see this behavior in its most concentrated form. You are interested in an item and are willing to pay $100. But when you see that someone has outbid you by fifty cents, it's hard not to bid $101, and so on until you end up buying the item for $200 because you couldn't bear losing by a margin defined in pennies. Becoming more conscious of what cues you to raise a financial stake will surface opportunities for effective microresolutions, perhaps resolving *to bid only twice on any one item*.

Spending to Impress Is Expensive

Do you ever order an expensive wine in a fancy restaurant because you feel intimidated by the waiter? Or buy the more expensive of two similar items proffered by a salesclerk because you're afraid he'll think you can't afford the pricier one? If asked by a hotel receptionist with a discriminating tone whether or not you would prefer to upgrade the budget room you reserved to a more luxurious accommodation, might you agree to pay the premium even though you had deliberately selected the least expensive room available when you booked?

Even very successful people can be made to feel like impostors in exclusive settings, overspending to keep themselves from being unmasked as pretenders to wealth. Studies conducted by researchers at Kellogg School of Management at Northwestern

University found that experiencing feelings of low status contributes to overspending and a willingness to pay more for an item.* Not surprisingly, professional sales and service people are expert at exploiting such feelings as a way to "upsell" a customer.

If you feel pressured to spend more than you'd budgeted, you might resolve to make your habitual response something like "That's more than I'd like to spend today" immediately upon being informed of the price, rather than giving yourself time to mull it over (or pretend to mull it over). Such a statement demonstrates control and confidence and gives the salesperson an opportunity to serve you within your budget. Yet deflating a salesperson's expectations can create feelings of awkwardness and even guilt.

In situations where you feel under mental pressure to behave against your own best interests, a microresolution message can be very effective. One of my favorite microresolution messages is the one Rachel came up with to help deflect the pressure she sometimes feels to make a purchase beyond her means: *It's okay to disappoint the salesperson.*

By giving herself this message when she feels pressured by a salesperson, Rachel is able to shift her mental focus away from her personal sense of financial inadequacy to the salesperson's motives and needs, defusing the embarrassment at not following through with an expensive purchase. The microresolution message or behavioral change you design for yourself will be personal to your own feelings of vulnerability in such situations (you might get more mileage out of a message such as *I don't need*

---

* D. D. Rucker and A. D. Galinsky, "Desire to Acquire: Powerlessness and Compensatory Consumption," *Kellogg Insight*, April 5, 2010.

to impress the salespeople to shop here). I've often noticed that people with very significant means are often cautious buyers, ask the most questions, and are more openly hostile to overpricing than those who fear being exposed as price conscious. Perhaps knowing that they can afford to buy almost any item frees them to consider whether or not the item is truly desirable, needed, or fairly priced. Those with less means may feel that if they ask too many questions or hesitate over the price, their financial status will be suspect. Thinking through the situations that cue feelings of unworthiness in "expensive" situations will help you figure out what resolutions you might make to free yourself from bad feelings and bad purchases.

Each of my spending microresolutions nudged my financial instincts in a saner direction, so that even those behaviors I hadn't directly targeted became more disciplined. But the biggest shift in my spending mindset came from a microresolution message I resolved to give myself when I was in danger of splurging on a glamorous but unnecessary item. Faced with the temptation to buy a luxurious article of clothing, the most expensive concert seats, or the latest and coolest electronic gadget, I would say to myself: *Security is the greatest luxury.*

Few things are as taxing to the spirit as financial worry, and the sumptuous feeling of a brand-new Prada handbag pales next to the luxury of knowing that you're financially secure. Increasing the top line is always desirable, but your spending habits should match your present financial situation, not what you expect (or hope) your earning power will be in the future. The dollars you part with today are worth more than the dollars you'll earn tomorrow, because what's in your wallet now has already been taxed. Even those who are naturally conservative in their financial habits can probably improve their spending behavior at the margin with little impact to their lifestyle. And if you think that your spending habits are such that they may endanger your long-term security, resolve to begin making discrete behavioral shifts that will put you on a more solid financial footing.

CHAPTER 16

Punctuality

My goodness how the time has flewn.
How did it get so late so soon?

—Dr. Seuss, "How Did It Get So Late So Soon?"

People with an on-time mindset believe that it's better to be ten minutes early than five minutes late, and for important meetings, better to be fifteen minutes early than *one minute* late. Those who strive for military precision call arriving early "on time" and arriving at the appointed hour "late."

I once showed up for a meeting at my firm fifteen minutes before the scheduled start. I arrived early because I was presenting and wanted to make sure that everything was in order before the meeting began. Five minutes before the hour, John Havens, then head of the powerful Equities Division (and later president of Citibank), came into the conference room. We chatted alone for several minutes as the clock ticked away. Five minutes after the hour, not a single person scheduled to attend a meeting of twenty people had yet arrived. "This is why it doesn't pay to show up on time for a meeting around here," I said to break the tension of watching a member of the firm's

Management Committee idling patiently. "Well," he said evenly, "my mother always told me that when you keep somebody waiting, you're basically saying to that person that your time is more valuable than his time, and it isn't. Everyone's time is equally valuable." Thinking to myself how often I ran late, I felt chastened by his remarks. As people began to drift in, it was clear from their alarmed expressions and the speed with which they scuttled into a seat that they hadn't expected Havens at the meeting, thinking that they would be keeping only lesser mortals waiting. The opposite of Havens's on-time principle was voiced by Oscar Wilde, who commented that "I am late on principle, the principle being that promptness is the thief of time"— meaning that if you're reasonably tardy, you won't have to waste your time waiting for latecomers.

I grew up in a late house. When my mother was scheduled to pick me up somewhere, she was nearly always late, sometimes by more than an hour. In an age before children could get an ETA via a quick cell-phone call, I can remember waiting for her in front of my elementary school, sitting on the school's sign, closing my eyes and counting, telling myself that when I reached one hundred and opened my eyes, I'd see her yellow station wagon headed up the school drive. Long after I had counted to a hundred a hundred times and my butt had begun aching from sitting on the narrow wooden sign, she'd pull up, and if I complained, my gentle mother would point out that perhaps I hadn't considered how much she had to do each day. One of my mother's greatest gifts was her deep generosity and spirit of tolerance, and I'm sure that was the lesson she meant to teach; in any case, for most of my life I found it hard to think of being ten minutes late as *late*.

In demonstrating how microresolutions can be used to improve on-time performance, it makes sense to divide lateness into two different categories: morning lateness and chronic lateness. While it is true that those who suffer from morning lateness may also be generally tardy, morning lateness merits its own discussion, as it so often results from actions taken (or untaken) the night before.

Morning Lateness

Failure to get to school, work, or a first appointment on time in the morning is the result of a series of behaviors that begin in the evening and culminate in a late departure the following morning. With respect to the hour of a morning arrival, the die is cast the night before. You may go to bed too late to get a good night's sleep so that when your alarm rings you hit the snooze button a few times too many before bolting from bed in a panic. If you didn't prepare for morning the evening before, you may lose precious minutes hunting for a clothing item, trying to find clean underwear in a sack of laundry not yet unpacked, printing out a document remembered too late, looking for keys you left in a jacket pocket when you walked the dog, or rooting around for something approximating sandwich bread for your kid's lunch. An extended example of a microresolution that addresses morning lateness can be found in chapter 5 ("Made to Measure"), but that's just a single demonstration of how microresolutions can help you to get where you're going on time and less harried.

Unless you want to get up earlier to create a wider margin for error and distractions, mornings really need to run like clockwork, on autopilot. Any action that isn't autopilot will have to be improvised, and improvisation is a very expensive activity. Anything you have to look for, fix, or amend in a routine is an improvisation, increases your stress level, and ups your chance of being late. Improvising requires rapid-fire decision making, which shares the same limited mental resources as self-control and initiative. All that unnecessary early-morning problem solving sends you out the door "ego depleted," to use researcher Roy Baumeister's phrase,* so before you've faced your first challenge at work or school, your mental resources are already ebbing. Mornings are all about routine—if you want to get a more consistent result, you'll have to build new habits and remake existing ones.

The hour you turn in to bed determines whether you'll be able to awake easily and with energy. If one of your issues is oversleeping, start there. No matter how many habits you build to grease the wheels of your morning departure, if you can't get out of bed at a reasonable time, you're going to be late. Read chapter 10 ("Sleep") to see how you might make a microresolution that gets you to bed earlier or allows you to sleep longer.

Be Prepared

Getting ready the evening before will speed your exit in the morning and allow you to sleep later (and perhaps more soundly) because most of the morning will already be in the bag. As discussed in chapter 10, it's an enormous time saver to wake up to clothes that have already been selected and prepared, but you have to build a routine for getting this done the night before. Prepacking briefcases and backpacks is also a function of habit, and if you are exiting with children, having a routine to make sure that they have packed everything that needs to go with them will spare you a ton of agitation in the first hour of your

---

* Roy F. Baumeister et al., "Ego Depletion: Is the Active Self a Limited Resource?" *Journal of Personality and Social Psychology* 74, no. 5 (1998): 1252–65.

day. There will always be occasional snafus, but most of our on-time efforts are undone by stumbling over ordinary and predictable tasks. Preparation is a core strategy for combating lateness, and the fifteen minutes it might take you to prepare in the evening are far less stressful than the fifteen it will take you in the morning. If it all sounds obvious, *it is*—just as it's obvious that to lose weight you have to eat less; it's obvious but not self-correcting. It requires rigor to change a behavior pattern, whether that pattern is eating late at night or hitting the snooze button on your alarm once too often.

Snooze and Lose

Sam had the habit of setting his alarm thirty minutes earlier than he needed to get up so that he could repeatedly hit the snooze button before rising. Building in so much snooze time often resulted in his dozing beyond the time he had meant to be his *real* wake-up call. The multiple snooze approach also meant that he might get up earlier or later on any given day, so there was no absolute reveille on which to hang a predictable morning routine. Realizing that his snooze strategy was hampering his on-time goals, Sam made a microresolution to have *zero tolerance for hitting the snooze button more than once on a weekday morning*. Instead, he set the alarm for five minutes before the drop-dead time to get up.

Lengthy snoozing can be a very hard habit to break (especially if you're not getting enough sleep), but after several weeks Sam began to appreciate the benefits of his new behavior. First, the twenty-five minutes of sleep that previously had been interrupted four times became a solid block, which was actually more restful than multiple snoozes. Second, building in time for only a single snooze dispelled the fuzziness around how late was too late (two snoozes, three, four?) and kept him from sleeping into the red zone. Finally, getting up at a consistent time made it possible for Sam to measure how much time he really needed to prepare to leave the house. Getting up at the same time every day makes it easier to get a bead on what other behaviors are contributing to a late exit.

Once you're out of bed and on the move, what trips you up? Taking too much time in the shower or blow-drying your hair? Looking for clothing items or changing your mind about what to wear? Breakfast? Packing lunches or briefcase or backpack? Kid or partner activities? An underfunded transit pass or an empty gas tank? Missing keys or a forgotten cell phone? You may not choose to build a habit for each one of these potential pitfalls, but making a series of microresolutions that pick off the top three will make a huge difference to your arriving on time and starting the day without a load of stress.

Once You Give Up Washing Your Hair, Everything Is a Piece of Cake

Washing and blow-drying my hair often put me behind in the morning. Getting up half an hour earlier two mornings a week was an unhappy event, and it was on these mornings that I was most likely to dawdle in bed and put myself behind. I wanted that extra thirty minutes of sleep, and I began to think of a way I could get the salon routine out of my mornings.

Trying to wash my hair the night before was a bust—I hated doing it at that hour, and it put a big dent in an evening that was already fully subscribed by family life, prep for the next day, and late-night work. So I rejiggered my exercise schedule at the gym so that it aligned with my hair-washing needs and resolved *to wash my hair immediately after my afternoon gym session*. As soon as I quit the gym floor I headed straight to the shower and doused my head, before I could talk myself into just going straight home. Getting hair washing out of the a.m. routine meant that every morning was cookie cutter, virtually no deviations unless something was forgotten or unprepared.

Running on Empty

Paul drove his child to school every day before heading into work. At least two mornings a month he found himself having to get gas on the way to school, invariably resulting in a late morning for both of them. While there were times when he was able to slip quickly in and out of the station, there were other times when there was a line at the pump or the credit-card reader said, "see attendant." Since he was operating under tremendous time pressure, Paul pumped in only a couple of gallons of gas, ensuring that another refueling stop would soon be needed.

Since both Paul and his wife used the car throughout the week, they noodled on a microresolution they could make that would ensure that there was always enough gas for the morning commute. They modeled their resolution on a nifty customer rule established by Zipcar—that cars must always be returned with at least a quarter tank of gas. Both Paul and his wife agreed never to return home with less than a quarter tank of fuel, which meant they each committed to making the same microresolution and following through with no excuses. As neither of them wanted to be the one caught out below the quarter-tank line and have to stop after work to refuel, both of them took more care to make sure the tank got topped up on the weekend.

Chronic Lateness

There's been a lot written about people who are chronically late, trying to isolate the psychological disposition that leads to nearly always showing up some minutes past the appointed hour. Some research points to lack of self-esteem, some to ego-tism; some studies say it's a power trip. Some psychology articles say that dawdling relieves anxiety, while others observe that those who are always early are overly anxious about being late. Still others speculate that tardy people are addicted to the rush—the challenge that comes from putting themselves in a squeeze.

Luckily, we can use microresolutions to reform the manifest behaviors that cause us to be late without understanding their exact psychological causes. Yet in isolating and addressing a be-havior pattern that contributes to tardiness, you may gain real insight into what drives you to be late when so much depends on being prompt.

Real Time

I suffer from very optimistic thinking when it comes to getting to an appointment on time. If I have plenty of time to get ready, I tend to first fill the extra time with other tasks, intending to stop and get ready while there is still ample time to prepare for depar-ture. Whether at work (where I might return phone calls, answer e-mail, or have an impromptu huddle before getting ready for my next meeting) or at home (where I might read the paper, answer e-mail, or do some work in the garden before getting ready), somehow I nearly always manage to find myself in a desperate rush to be on time, turning even comfortable appointment times into cliff-hangers. Since I clearly am unrealistic in assessing the time required to get ready, I've decided to reorder my behavior so that less depends on my ability to estimate.

My new resolution is *to get ready first, with single-minded purpose*. If I have an hour available to prepare before a business appointment and I think I need only fifteen minutes to get ready, I prepare immediately, researching, organizing materials, getting last-minute details from others, and freshening up, rather than waiting until fifteen minutes before the meeting to prep. If it's the weekend and I need to leave the house in forty-five minutes to go to my Pilates class, I dress and pack up before doing anything unrelated to departure, even if I think it's only going to take me ten minutes to get ready—that's the *prepare first* part of my resolution; *single-minded purpose* means that I table any ideas/needs/tasks that enter my mind while I'm getting ready, and that's difficult for me. I don't answer calls, texts, or e-mails while getting ready, even if I'm almost ready and it looks like I have time to spare. If my single-minded pursuit of "ready" results in my finishing early, I set the timer on my phone to ring at the moment I have to leave, and when the timer goes off, I get up and walk straight out. Though it's still early days, I've already learned a lot since I began practicing my new resolution.

Preparing first exposes how much time it really takes to get ready. On some occasions when I thought I had so much time that I'd be ready and twiddling my thumbs, it turned out that there wasn't a moment to spare. What's your working definition of "ready"? When I call upstairs to my kid, "Ready?" and she enthusiastically calls back, "Yes!" any or all of the following may be true: no shoes, no socks, face unwashed, hair not brushed; glasses, coat, hat, gloves, or scarf missing; items that need to come along not yet packed up. As adults our notion of "ready" may be more comprehensive but still incomplete. You really aren't "ready" until everything that is leaving with you is packed up and can just be scooped up on the way out. You can be completely dressed, but if you have to look up the appointment address or map it before leaving, you're not yet ready; if you just have to strap on your watch, you're not yet ready; if you have to retrieve your charger from under the bed, you're not yet ready. It's our incomplete definition of "ready" that so often is responsible for our being late.

The more time I have to prepare, the harder it is for me to stay on track and the more tempted I am to interrupt myself with other tasks. In contrast, if the time to get ready is very limited, I'm far less likely to get involved in something that puts me behind, because it's obvious there isn't enough time. Perhaps the method in the madness of waiting until the last minute to get ready is that the sudden urgency created shuts down internal noise and forces concentration.

Appointments, like any hard stop, create a before and after in the day. This is true whether one is getting ready for a single appointment or a series of meetings that won't conclude until day's end. As soon as we begin preparing for that hard stop, we have to accept the limits of what we managed to achieve and what will remain undone, perhaps for many hours. A departure forces a break in work flow and exposes deficits in one's organizational habits overall—only when we're almost out of time do we realize that there are several small but important tasks that need handling. You can see this phenomenon clearly when you prepare to go on vacation and you realize that all those mundane tasks you put off until "tomorrow" can't wait two weeks, so now they're urgent. The lesson? The more organizational behaviors you can build into autopilot, the less frantic your departures, large and small, will be (see chapter 17, "Organization").

It's still early days for my new lateness resolutions, but I'm making a lot of progress, my on-time rate has improved tremendously, and when I am late I'm much closer to the mark. What a relief it is not to arrive with an apology or, worse, an explanation. A friend of mine took this idea further by making a microresolution never to give an excuse for being late. "My excuses were meaningless," she told me, "because I was always late. Once I'm behind, anything that doesn't break my way seems like a valid excuse for arriving late. For me it was important to stop thinking that just about anything is a reasonable justification for keeping someone waiting. Since I resolved never to give myself an excuse or explain, I'm more focused on being on time, and if I'm late at least I don't have to hear myself go on forever about the trains."

My friend's remark about being late because of bad breaks will resonate with many of the tardy. The late depend on luck—catching the train at the last second, finding the perfect parking space, no line at the ATM. The unlate assume the unexpected—transit delays, detours, difficulty finding an address—and account for it in calculating how much time they'll need to safely arrive on time.

Showing up late can damage you both personally and professionally. But like every other area of self-improvement, lateness is a result of ingrained habits and attitudes that can be altered through the rigorous drilling of new behaviors. Giving your focus exclusively to changing an attitude through messaging or a single behavior through practice will begin to shrink the margin by which you habitually run behind. It's never too late to learn to be on time!

CHAPTER 17

Organization

> Chaos was the law of nature; Order was the dream of man.
>
> —Henry Adams

Neatness is the physical side of managing clutter; organization, the mental side. If you're organized, you can bring a clear mind and your best game to your personal and professional life. Organization enables you to lay your hands on what you need when you need it, whether that's a document on a computer, a phone number, meeting minutes, a birth certificate, or an umbrella. Organization enables you to show up prepared, on time, and in the right place. Organization enables the effective and active management of an ever-changing demand set at work and at home, so top priorities receive the most attention and minor tasks don't become emergencies. Organization enables you to refresh your memory on the important details of projects, meetings, phone calls, conferences. Organization is a mindset that reminds you of the importance of delegating effectively and early.

You can create the planet's cleverest prioritization or filing scheme, but if you do not painstakingly build habits to support it, it will be a failure. Organization is a set of systems that, like its close cousin neatness, depends entirely on autopilot for success. Annual pledges *to be organized* (always on the top-ten New Year's resolution list) drive wannabe organizers into container, closet, and organizer outlets in the belief that the key to success is a multicompartment desk organizer. There's nothing wrong with inspiring yourself with a pyramid of slots and cubbyholes, as long as you recognize that until you build the habits that steer the right item into the right slot at the right time, you won't really have a system you can maintain without mental effort.

A naturally logical and organized mind is a gift, as is the ability to operate effectively in chaos, but even if you can store, sift, and sort details in your head while bullets fly, getting better organized will save you time, stress, creative energy, and self-control. Whenever you have to hunt for items, make panic preparations for a forgotten appoinment, or spend fifteen minutes looking for meeting minutes on your computer or ten minutes going through a pile of mail looking for a scary notice you saw two or three weeks ago, you're burning that precious resource known as active initiative, part of the limited mental-resource pool shared with self-control and decision making. If you spend ten minutes looking for a document in a pile on your desk, then search for it in your online calendar in case it was an attachment to a meeting, and finally end up calling a colleague for a copy, your active-initiative store will be at low ebb by the time you finally lay your hands on it and head into the conference room. In contrast, if you can process predictable tasks mindlessly via autopilot, you preserve your best thinking for your most challenging work. Why waste ingenuity and heroic effort on routine tasks?

The microresolutions method is itself an organizational tool kit that helps you isolate a behavioral change that brings results. Home in on a single change in habit that will save you time and make you more effective. The change should not be comprehensive or complex; it need only move what is now a psychologically effortful activity into autopilot. Pinpoint just one organizational element that needs addressing and make it the subject of your next microresolution. For example, if you regularly stress out while searching for notes and documents required for your next meeting, think through exactly why these documents prove difficult to locate. Do you have to search for them in piles? Are there multiple versions on your computer (and/or laptop) that you have to sort through to find the final version? Did you take notes on a presentation that ended up at home? Is your filing system so general that the document might have ended up in several different categories? After thinking through the shortfalls in your current document-management system (or lack thereof), you might decide that your biggest issue is finding materials and minutes for meetings past. You might resolve to put important notes taken at a meeting in the electronic calendar entry or to create a chronological file for any documents presented at a meeting so that you can easily find and review them. Such a habit would give you confidence that you at least have a well-organized chronological file of key meeting documents and notes. Sustaining such a system would require a no-excuses resolution to file notes within a limited window of time following the meeting or at a given time each day; to get started you might limit your new system to a single important meeting series so that you can begin building a habit and experiencing benefits while limiting obstacles.

Any system you create for yourself will be only as strong as the habits you build to support it, so start with a simple system and elaborate it as needed over time. If you go from no filing system to something as elaborate as the Dewey decimal system, you are going to fail. But it's amazing how creating a single simple organizational habit can make you more productive.

We Have Contact

Zach loved his smart phone and depended on it both personally and professionally. Each week he received many calls from numbers not on his contact list. He seldom added a new number to his list immediately, preferring to wait until the contact proved to be of lasting value. When Zach needed to find a number he hadn't yet made an official contact, he would hunt through the list of calls received, often listening to several voice mails before locating the right number. Because he used his voice-mail archive as a shadow contact list (a sort of contact purgatory for numbers not yet promoted to permanent status), his voice-mail box was often filled to capacity.

Zach made a microresolution *to add every new caller to my contact list immediately with zero tolerance for delay.* Rather than deciding which numbers were worth converting to contacts, he began creating a contact record for every new number as soon as he finished a call or listened to a voice mail. Although he was often in a hurry and tempted to create the contact later in the day, the *zero-tolerance* framing of his resolution kept him from delaying. Zach became ultrafast at adding a new contact with just enough name info to make it recognizable, the whole process taking less than thirty seconds per record.

This change in habit immediately upped Zach's productivity. No scanning call lists and trying to figure out if the call from the dentist was the call that came in at 11:00 a.m. or 11:15 a.m. No listening to scores of voice messages in order to locate a phone number while time was tight to make a call. No more missed phone messages because voice mail was full. Even taking time to add the numbers of organizations he didn't want to be in contact with was useful, since it enabled Zach to avoid answering such calls in the future.

In-box Overload

Elaine had a secretary who maintained a filing system for her that kept her desk at work fairly clear, but her desk at home was heaped with papers. The stack contained unopened mail, catalogs, magazines, receipts, bills pending, things to read, important documents to keep, items to take action on. Elaine used her memory to keep track of what was in the pile and what needed attention, often conducting frantic searches for documents that required action (yesterday).

Looking at her desk, Elaine saw that much of the bulk in the pile was junk mail, catalogs, and magazines. In trying to reduce the pile on her desk, she resolved *to cull mail before I bring it into the apartment.* Instead of just taking the contents of the mailbox and adding it to the stack on her desk, she would stand by the recycling bin in the back hall and toss out junk mail and catalogs, cutting the pile by two-thirds or more. Elaine began leaving the magazines on the coffee table in the living room before dropping the remaining mail on her desk.

The pile was smaller, but items requiring action often languished for weeks, until they became emergencies. Elaine's second desk microresolution was to establish administrative action days on the first and third Monday of every month. Monday was a good day to do the bills, because her boyfriend had a class on Monday nights and she was always on her own. Doing administrative work every two weeks kept the pile manageable and kept her from worrying that she was missing something.

Elaine added yet a third microresolution after months of working her first two: *to open all mail before placing it in the action basket.* She had discovered that a couple of letters that looked like routine bills actually were time-sensitive communications that required immediate action, but she hadn't realized it until she reviewed them on admin night. Elaine's new resolution took only a few minutes a day and ensured that she caught those rare action items that simply couldn't wait.

Elaine's three microresolutions show how organizational systems evolve over time with experience and how each new system must be drilled before it takes hold. Once a new system is fully operational, it's easier to see what other systems could be instituted to enhance one's effectiveness.

Nothing to Fear but Fear Itself

Katherine, a senior attorney at a federal agency, was charged with bringing some of the government's most important cases. She managed a dynamic priority list that always included a list of phone calls to be made. Among those calls there was nearly always one that she dreaded making because she expected it would cause discord, confrontation, or distress. The *scary call* was not always the most urgent call casewise, so it was easy to let it slide. But Katherine noticed that whenever she had such a call to make, it loomed over all of her other activities, draining her initiative and rendering her less productive, and by that measure the *scary call* was the most important call on the list to make.

Katherine made a microresolution *to always make the scary*

call first. No matter what other calls were on the list, she got the call she didn't want to make over with first. "I am more productive and much, much happier at work since I made my resolution. As soon as I get the scary call out of the way I get a huge surge of energy that carries me through the rest of the day. It's not that the scary call was the only thing I ever put off doing, but it was the thing I put off doing most consistently and now I never put it off. It's the first thing I do each day, no matter what."

Katherine's resolution is a good model for a microresolution focused on priorities. So often we think of the item with the most business impact as the highest priority, but there are other yardsticks, such as the *scary call.* Another yardstick of priority you might consider is whether or not an item requires action from others. When you delay delegating a project or breaking it up among several contributors, you put everybody behind before they start. Making a microresolution *to elevate all delegation decisions to the top of the priority list* will keep you from having to make a slew of apologetic calls at the last minute while looking incompetent at the same time. For some, routine administrative work is so dreaded that it languishes at the bottom of the priority list until it becomes urgent. If you're chronically late with simple administrative tasks, resolving to get them done the day they hit your in-box will help your professional profile and overall productivity. Each resolution will take considerable practice to institutionalize: You can't just do it a couple of times; you have to drill it to make it stick.

Every small uptick in organizational skills saves time, prevents panic, and preserves active-initiative stores for problem solving, creativity, and decision making.

Redefining the Hour

Cindy's schedule was often crowded with large blocks of back-to-back meetings. Tasks that needed doing between meetings—answering e-mail, returning phone calls, checking in with team members on progress—often put her behind so that by afternoon she was running ten to fifteen minutes late. The items that couldn't be squeezed in between meetings were forced into the evening hours.

Cindy made a microresolution to schedule all hourlong meetings under her control for fifty minutes and to reduce half-hour meetings to twenty-five minutes. The slightly shorter meeting blocks gave her (and the others who attended her meetings) a margin of time to catch up on calls and e-mails and to schedule urgent conversations that couldn't wait until the end of the day. As Cindy was the owner of about half the meetings she attended, she ended up with about forty minutes of buffer time per day that she hadn't had before.

The new scheduling meant that Cindy kept more on top of her workload during the day, getting items handled or delegated before they became urgent, and there was less left to catch up on in the evenings. Further, the slightly shorter meetings became more focused and productive. Lest you think that all of this has nothing to do with habit, think again—it's habit to use a full hour to discuss a topic, and autopilot will often take you to the last minute of the hour in the same way that it will lead you to clean your plate, because that's what's routine. Making all meetings fifty minutes is almost like learning new math, thinking and operating in base fifty instead of base sixty.

Until I made my most recent on-time resolution (*to prepare first with single-minded purpose*), I would generally show up for my Pilates class around eight minutes late. Once I began arriving on time, the class seemed very, very long. I kept looking up at the clock expecting the class to be over, and yet there were still ten minutes left to go. My chronic lateness had adjusted my mindset so that my "hour" of exercise was really closer to fifty minutes, around 18 percent less than the full hour. It took weeks of on-time arrivals before my mindset "workout hour" realigned to sixty minutes. Mindsets reflect habit, and they change as our habits change.

To Do or Not to Do

Derek has a busy full-time job and is also responsible for managing and contributing to a family business. His workday often extends well into the evening, either continuing work from his job or picking up on family business that couldn't be handled during the day. Derek dutifully kept a comprehensive list of business action items for both his day job and his family's farm. These items ranged from the trivial to the urgent, from writing a report to clearing out a barn. Despite carefully capturing all the action items so that he wouldn't lose track, he often felt overwhelmed and wasn't always sure where to put most of his attention.

Derek made a microresolution *to maintain a separate page in his notebook for his top three priorities.* He began selecting his top three from his to-do list each morning as the first order of business when he arrived at his office, but he found that as soon as he set foot in the office he was driven by events and didn't always have time to settle his list. So Derek tuned his resolution: *to select three priorities for tomorrow as my last task of today.*

Derek found designating priorities at the end of the workday to be much more effective. More relaxed in the evening than in the morning, he found he had a sharper perspective on what was most important. Reestablishing the priorities just before leaving work gave him a clear direction going into the next day. He slept better and awoke with more energy, both unanticipated benefits of separating his top priorities from his lengthy to-do list.

. . . Until the Fat Lady Sings

I'd like to close this chapter's microresolution examples with one made by Helen, my thirteen-year-old daughter, who prepares all typewritten assignments on a laptop in her bedroom. The printer is on the floor below her room, so Helen fell into the habit of printing all her work in a batch at the end of her homework session, often just before bed. Since the typewritten homework might have been completed hours earlier, she would sometimes forget to print a homework assignment and remember only in the morning, making her late for school. Other times, something as simple as a printer jam or ink-cartridge issue would cost her thirty minutes of sleep.

Helen made a microresolution to print out each assignment as she completed it, even though that meant running up and downstairs several times rather than making a single trip at the end of the evening. This resolution kept her from forgetting to print documents and from losing sleep due to late-night printer snafus, ensuring that when she finished her last assignment of the evening she was truly and completely *done*.

But What About One-off Projects?

Microresolutions are designed to help you drill new behavior until it becomes habit, but the same microresolution rules that build better behaviors into autopilot can also be applied to one-off projects—cleaning out the garage, selling old items on the Internet, finishing photo albums, writing thank-you notes—that either never get started or never get completed.

Have you ever had the following experience? You have Sunday free and you embark on a project to clean out a closet, and you attack it with tremendous energy and enthusiasm. Your aim is to cull, sort, and reorganize the items in the closet so that there is more space and items are easier to locate, and you're willing to spend the entire day and evening to reach your goal. The closet is full of shoes that need fixing and clothing that is either in poor repair or years unworn; there are sundry items stacked on the upper shelves. You remove everything from the closet—the hanging items, shoes, and boxes—and begin sorting and discarding, making piles on the floor or bed. A pile for clothes that need cleaning, another for those that need repair, another for those to give away or sell, another for those that are so rarely worn they should be stored away. By Sunday evening you're exhausted but nowhere close to finishing your project. The items on the bed need to be shifted to chairs in order to sleep, and clothing for work the next day needs to be rescued from the pile. After several days of living in chaos, you return the majority of items to the closet without reorganization. It's a year or two before you try again.

Just as a personal-improvement goal means changing multiple habits and attitudes, the closet (or basement or garage) initiative is actually several projects, each requiring a discrete focus. In order to comply with the microresolution rules, each of these micro projects must be limited and measurable and provide an immediate benefit. For example, going through all the shoes in your closet and discarding those that you won't ever wear again can probably be accomplished in fifteen minutes. It might take half an hour to drop off shoes needing repair at the shoemaker. Each of these actions is a separate project, and each provides a unique and immediate benefit. Removing unwanted shoes will make it easier to find shoes you'll actually wear; repairing shoes means expanding footwear choices.

Such discrete organizational projects can be handled within an hour, some in as little as five minutes. Reorganizing your entire desk space could be a big job; removing all the items from the desk drawer that shouldn't be there is a valuable and manageable goal. These same guidelines work when doing your taxes or applying for a new job. The key is never to begin a project unit that you can't finish in a limited amount of time or allow yourself to become overwhelmed. There's no point in going at it until you're exhausted and complete project aversion sinks in. Stick with the limited and achievable, and you'll have energy for the long run.

"*But,*" you might say, "*you can't get the bigger organizational picture in a closet if you work a shelf at a time—it might be that some items on the top shelf really belong on the shelf below, but you can only see that when you consider the whole.*" Working in situ limits the big picture but prevents chaos from taking hold and project completion horizons from expanding. After you've culled and organized each closet section on its own, you'll more easily be able to think through what to do on a macro level with the remaining items in the closet. By that time, you won't be dealing with any closet noise; everything in the closet will be a keeper and in a more logical grouping.

Tackling a large project the microresolution way—nailing one benefit at a time—will help you sustain your energy and enthusiasm while improving your life immediately. Don't just dive in; figure out a reasonable unit of work that will provide a benefit, commit to it, and execute immediately.

Nano Resolutions

Big projects often don't get done because they loom large; small projects often don't get done because they don't attract enough attention. These are not the daily to-dos you expect to cross off your list or habits you need to build, but the nonurgent, pesky maintenance tasks that we sometimes let ride for months, if not years. Each of these tasks takes little time to complete, but in the aggregate they can be overwhelming. Oiling a squeaky hinge, sewing tassels back on a couch pillow, changing a lightbulb that requires a ladder, vacuuming the interior of a car, gluing the broken handle back onto a favorite mug, straightening a kitchen drawer. Most of us have a grab bag of tiny projects waiting to be done, hovering at the edge of consciousness and contributing to stress (every time that hinge squeaks).

You can take care of mini one-off projects that can be completed in ten minutes or less with a *nano resolution*. A nano resolution follows the core microresolution principles: easy, limited, precise, measurable, immediate benefits. Just like its bigger cousin, a nano requires an ironclad commitment, but it's over in ten minutes, whereas a microresolution runs for weeks in order to institute a repeatable behavior.

I keep a list in my notebook of all the nanos I might choose to do if I find myself with ten minutes or want to take a break from a longer task, such as writing this book. My nano list has all manner of tasks—sewing a button onto a pair of pants; listing a used book for sale on Amazon; collecting a box full of neglected toys from my daughter's room and putting them out on the stoop for the neighborhood children to take; screwing in the screw that fell out of my closet doorknob; reading an article a friend sent me a week ago. Again, the nanos aren't on my regular to-do list of items that need to get done daily or weekly; they're floating items that are important in their way but not particularly time sensitive. For example, I wouldn't put an item to write a thank-you note on my nano list, because a thank-you note needs to be prompt.

When I have a little time or I want to take a break from working, watching, or surfing, I take a look at my nano list and pick a project. As with any resolution in the micro family, once you commit, you're in no-excuses territory—you're on the hook to get it done. Knowing that it's only going to take ten minutes keeps focus high and inertia at bay. It's immensely satisfying to nail a nano on an impulse, and sometimes it feels like the most productive thing I've done all day (and it might be, if it's Sunday).

I keep a list, but a nano resolution can be utterly impromptu. You can make a snap decision to nano something, but you have to bring focus and commitment for the ten minutes it takes to complete. For example, if you decide that you're going to repot a plant in the garden, go right for it and don't let yourself get distracted until it's done. When you walk into the garden you'll see other things that need doing—perhaps one of the rosebushes needs pruning or a geranium needs watering. Don't let yourself get distracted for a single second from your commitment; get your nano done before you consider doing another thing. As long as you stay focused, you can straighten out almost any drawer in ten minutes, create some new files in five minutes, change the washer in the kitchen sink in three minutes (or call the plumber in one minute).

For me, knocking off a nano is a kind of treat, a break from must-do work, a stress reliever that demonstrates that a better quality of life just depends on targeted focus and commitment at the margin.

Afterword: Beyond Autopilot

> Watch your thoughts; they become words.
> Watch your words; they become actions.
> Watch your actions; they become habits.
> Watch your habits; they become character.
> Watch your character; it becomes your destiny.
>
> —Lao-tzu

By now perhaps you've already given your first microresolution a try; maybe it has already become habit. If you're still at the stage where your target behavior feels awkward, don't despair; soon your new habit will feel more natural, and further down the road it will become second nature. Once in autopilot, your behavior will sustain itself, marking the conclusion of the microresolution life cycle. But is autopilot an end or a beginning?

Despite the fact that most behavior is unconscious routine, we don't think of ourselves as passive creatures of habit. Rather, we think of ourselves as decision makers exercising free will and making conscious choices. We believe that what we do is what we choose to do—what we like to do. Our habits are aligned with preferences that keep us believing that even routine behaviors are deliberate choices. Although some habits grow out of preferences—developing a taste for Frappuccinos, for example—it's just as often the other way around: Our preferences develop as a result of our habits.

Take the case of a child learning to brush her teeth. The parent leads the child to the washbasin night after night to supervise the forging of this essential habit. At some point, the child learns to brush without supervision, but it may take far longer for her to actually want to brush. Yet at some point the child begins to brush because she prefers clean, slick teeth to sour, scummy ones. Had she not been taught the tooth-brushing habit, her unbrushed teeth would feel normal, preferable. The adult preference for clean teeth develops as a direct result of the relentless practice of this childhood habit.

Teeth flossing was introduced after my father's childhood dental-care training, and he once peevishly told his dentist that he didn't like flossing and didn't do it regularly. "That's okay," said the dentist, "just floss the teeth you want to keep." Startled into action by the dentist's deadpan wit (*who knew?*), my father began flossing, complaining every time he forced himself to do it. At some point he discovered that he loved flossing and said that his teeth "itched" if he didn't do it. Flossed teeth became his new normal, the state he preferred.

A person who has always been active and played sports can't imagine an inactive lifestyle, but for others, exercise is something they must learn to love. A sedentary person embarking on a cycling program may view each ride as a dreaded chore, but if the routine is maintained over time, the couch potato is likely to become a devoted cyclist. Going for a bike ride becomes a relaxation preferable to collapsing into a chair with the Sunday paper for two hours (well, most of the time).

Preference is habit's powerful ally, giving an aura of volition and inclination to autopilot activity. Preference keeps us from seeing that most of our "choices" are practiced responses. The foods we eat, our communication style, and the general manner in which we do things appear to us as conscious, considered choices, not mindless patterns. Each time we defend our preferences, we reinforce our habits. And once we succeed in making a change in habit, we often find that our old preferences stick around, suddenly out of sync with our new behavior.

Like the ghosts of habits past, old preferences haunt us months, even years, after we've made a lasting change in our behavior. These lingering preferences create nostalgia for the old habits and attitudes we worked so hard to shed, whispering to us that we should stop kidding ourselves; we would really rather eat a cookie than a bowl of strawberries, rather stay up late watching a series rerun than go to bed and get a good night's sleep, rather score a point by one-upping a colleague than strengthen an alliance with a show of support. Even after experiencing the rich benefits of a new habit, it often takes us longer to embrace it as a true preference.

Preferences are part of our identity, how we describe and think about ourselves. Years ago I gave up caffeine as part of a diet plan, never expecting to stick with it beyond reaching my weight-loss goal. I loved coffee, I loved caffeine, and I had mild contempt for sissies ordering decaf. But once I went through the discomfort of caffeine withdrawal and began waking up with energy in place of lethargy, I decided to make my shift to decaffeinated drinks permanent. I was happy to be free of my addiction, but I hated being "a decaf person," because "decaf" didn't match the image I had of myself as someone who thrived on high-octane fuel. I liked my new behavior but not my new identity (*coffee sissy*).* My silly (and temporary) identity crisis illustrates how even a small change in habit can be a challenge to self-image.

Families and friends may also view a change in a person's habits as a change in identity. Families cultivate and share a unique identity based on their culture of rituals, beliefs, and values. It's unnerving (and threatening) to the clan when a member breaks with its traditions (shared habits), even if those traditions aren't particularly healthy. If you come home eating brown rice in place of white and passing on the second round of beer, you may put family members on the defensive and find yourself apologizing for having changed your tastes.

As we grow into adults, we continue to identify ourselves through a variety of preferences and habits, even trivial or negative ones. *I'm lazy, I'm a spendthrift, I'm a doormat, I'm a sweet freak, I'm such a slob, I'm a Gleek*. On Facebook we express our identity in terms of what we like to read, listen to, and watch. In the wonderful David Rabe play *Hurlyburly*, the character Donna announces herself at an impromptu party by declaring: "Drugs are and just have been as far as I can remember an ever-present component of my personality. . . . *I am a drug person*." † As it must be true that Donna acquired her drug habit at a point beyond her earliest childhood, her description of drugs as an "ever-present component" of her personality demonstrates how we can confuse entrenched habits with immutable identity.

The role of preference in identity answers the question I posed in the preface to this book: Why do I continue to hang

---

* I recently read that in some artisanal coffee shops my order of a decaf skim latte is known as a "Why Bother?"
† David Rabe, *Hurlyburly* (Samuel French, 1976) (emphasis added).

up my car keys at my parents' house when it no longer makes any practical sense? Well, hanging up keys in my childhood home is not just a habit, not just a preference, but a ritual that is a part of my identity—in our family we hang up our keys as soon as we come home. Following the old family rule comforts and pleases me, makes me feel—literally—*at home*. The linkage among behavior, preference, and identity is powerful stuff. That's why a change in behavior is so difficult and why, even after we have succeeded in changing ourselves, we sometimes have to give our mindset a bit of time to catch up.

The habits you are building through microresolutions will ultimately give birth to new preferences. After a bit more time than it takes to move a behavior into autopilot, your preferences will realign with your new habits, and nostalgia for old routines will fade away. You'll find that you prefer to make the bed, stop eating before you feel stuffed, walk instead of ride, refrain from having the last word, sleep instead of shop on the Internet, eat dinner without checking your smart phone, pay bills on time, roller-skate rather than watch television. This, finally, is where there really is no turning back on the new behaviors that you've taught yourself, because those new habits now enjoy the status of esteemed preferences.

As your preferences shift to support your new habits, your sense of who you are will shift too. You'll discover that the experience of doing things in a new way has made a different person of you. You'll begin to identify with your new behaviors, to describe yourself differently. You'll realize that you are indeed improved—in fact, transformed. A change in *doing* has made a change in *being*. Learning how to do just one thing differently punches your ticket for a voyage of continuous personal progress.

Ralph Waldo Emerson called it "the endless work of self-improvement," and indeed the desire to become a better self is a universal human urge. The longer we keep up our quest, the longer we stay young, because self-discovery and self-invention are essential qualities of youth. We associate old age with rigidity, with the grumpy senior citizen who insists that the right way to do something is the way he learned to do it long ago. But if you make self-improvement a way of life, you'll be practicing the flexibility and self-invention that accounts for so much of the vibrancy of youth.

Whatever your age and aspirations, transformation is within your reach, you just need to invest in the everyday process that works the magic. Like Dorothy, who sought help from a great and powerful wizard only to find that she already possessed the power to reach her destination, you alone have the power to transport yourself. A single shift in behavior or attitude will take you to a brand-new place without a pair of ruby slippers; all you need to do is chart your course. You don't need a wand or hocus-pocus—just focus.

The great nineteenth-century writer George Eliot (born Mary Ann Evans) authored some of the English language's most thrilling stories of personal self-discovery and transformation. A late bloomer who wrote her first book at forty and married at sixty-one, she once famously said, "It's never too late to be who we might have been."

Acknowledgments

I owe the publication of *Small Move, Big Change* to a series of serendipitous events that began when I told Margaret Beels over breakfast about the book I was then calling *Microresolutions*. Margaret listened politely and that evening dropped me an e-mail to say that she "had a friend in the publishing industry" willing to read an excerpt and give me feedback.

I got in contact with Margaret's friend Stephen Morrison without really understanding who he was. I sent Stephen an excerpt of my book late on a Friday night and to my astonishment, I heard back from him before 8:00 a.m. on Saturday morning. It turned out that Stephen was the new head of Picador Press, and he offered me encouragement, guidance, and introductions to agents. Stephen's interest in my book was like a magic wand that transformed me from an unknown aspirant into a writer with a promising property.

Once Stephen introduced me to my delightful agent, Stephanie Cabot of The Gernert Company, events accelerated, with Stephanie guiding me through the formal proposal stage, meetings with publishers, and finally the auction for the book, all within the space of about six weeks. I profited immensely from Stephanie's good taste, judgment, and true friendship. Thanks also to Stephanie's intrepid assistant, Anna Worall, whose cheery competence and insightful comments were often a boon to me during the dog days of this project.

Margaret, Stephen, and Stephanie helped me to get lucky in a business where luck is rare. And what a stroke of luck it was to land Wendy Wolf of Viking as my editor! Wendy's edits were scribbled in a physician-like hand that was almost impossible to read, but once deciphered offered clear prescriptions for idea enrichment and a more disciplined message that taken in aggregate resulted in a far stronger book than I originally submitted. (The only word I could ever read at a glance in Wendy's handwriting was "UGH.") Margaret Riggs, Wendy's assistant editor, kept the process on track and details from falling through the cracks.

The superb production team at the Penguin Random House then worked their professional magic on my humble Word file to transform it into a real book. Nancy Sheppard, Viking's marketing director, set the book's commercial course and helped me understand how I might distinguish my book in a crowded marketplace. Vice president and publicity director Carolyn Coleburn, whose intelligence and good humor I remembered well from my proposal meeting, deployed the outstanding publicity team of Shannon Twomey and Cat Boyd to promote the book. Shannon and Cat expertly worked their network to get the book broad exposure, smartly organized tour events, and wisely counseled me on personal appearances. Viking's creative director Paul Buckley and his team managed to capture the power of a microresolution in a single, imaginative cover image. Noirin Lucas, assistant director of copy editing, ensured through her meticulous revisions that I didn't put a comma wrong or, worse, erroneously attribute a quote. Senior marketing manager Paul Lamb counseled me on ways to present my work online and in social media, helping me distill the tweet-size messages that would carry the greatest power. While making a print book turned out to be a longer process that I had ever imagined, the gang at Viking Penguin made it worth the wait.

Throughout every stage of this project there were friends and family who contributed to its success. My sister Jane Halsey, a wonderful copy editor of books much more important than my own, made the awkward graceful and the plodding soar in the critical early drafts. My brother Oliver Arnold, a professor of Shakespeare at Berkeley, was my first reader and helped me shape the book proposal whose deadline occurred in the midst of our joint family vacation. Writer and journalist (and legal lecturer and New York governor's aide) Adam Cohen was my shadow adviser on the world of publishing and my brainstorming partner on the long walks we took together weekly. Maria Mazer and Linda Badger were early readers whose critical feedback improved my efforts and whose encouragement kept me tapping away. My father, Maxwell Arnold, a very classy and economical writer who died before the publication of this book, read the manuscript in a single sitting, recording razor sharp edits in a shaky hand.

I am grateful to my husband, Shan Sullivan, who suffered through a year of dinners that somehow always turned into microresolution think tanks. His critical questioning helped sharpen my thinking while his validations boosted my spirit and gave me the confidence to stick with it.

Although my sabbatical year as a writer was unnerving to my daughter, Helen, who preferred a Wall Street mom in pinstripes to an ink-stained mom in sweatpants, Helen became a micro-resolutions convert and surprised me a number of times by giving me very good edits while reading over my shoulder (such comments nearly always began, "Mommy, you can't say that!").

Acknowledgments

Finally, deep and heartfelt thanks to all the micro-resolvers whose engaging human stories form the bedrock of this book. Their successes convinced me that committing the microresolution system to paper was indeed worthwhile, perhaps even important.

Index

Index

Index